Ask a stupid question!

Ask a stupid question!

A personal development guide on how to ask better questions

Andrew Griffiths

This edition was published in 2012 by Andrew Griffiths, PSL Consultants Ltd, UK.

ISBN: 978 0 9571775 0 5

Printed in the Great Britain by Lightning Source
Typesetting and Cover Design by www.wordzworth.com

Foreword

Thank you for picking up this book. I believe that what follows will be useful to you. Flick through if you like and see what catches your eye – although I've told the story as a kind of journey, reflecting my own, so it helps to start at the beginning.

The book is intended to explain itself so I shall not say too much in this foreword. One of the difficulties I had in writing it was knowing quite where to start on a subject that is constantly intriguing and amazing. I have learned first-hand about the great power of good questioning skills. But more important than this, for me, I have learned over a number of years that there is a way that this power can be harnessed readily by all of us in every walk of life. That is what I intend to share in the pages that follow.

I also had to find a language and a style that would appeal to a broad audience. Everyone really who can read and wants to develop their potential, assert themselves and learn how to live, cope and thrive in a very complex world.

I do not use too many business terms because I think this book has lasting value while many business terms are short-lived or have varied meaning in different business tribes. I felt the book therefore deserved to be written simply and as clearly as I can contrive.

Apart from which, as I say, the book is not just for people in business or seeking better employment – we can all sell, lead, influence, perform, seek to work better and so on. It is for anyone who wants to achieve more for themselves and others.

Contents

Chapter One

Why do we need this book?

Because by asking the right questions skilfully we can transform our lives.

Questions are an essential tool of communication in any situation. They can be extremely powerful and can lead individuals and organisations to achieve dramatic improvements, find much-needed solutions, and introduce world-leading innovations. It doesn't matter how young or old you are, where you come from or what you do in life, if you develop your questioning skills you will achieve and gain more.

A good question can transform the course of a personal or professional relationship; it can open doors, ignite creative thinking, instil trust, establish dialogue – it can make people think about what's possible and achievable. Just think what followed after the 52 year-old travelling salesman, Ray Kroc, the man behind the fast-food chain, McDonalds, asked himself, "Where can I get a good hamburger on the road?" Then wonder at the phenomenal scientific advances that have been made since James Watson and Francis Crick queried, "What might DNA look like in a 3D form?"

Behind most 'Eureka' moments, we do not find the great inventors, researchers and scientists suddenly unveiling the bright light of truth, so much as finding the right question to ask that will lead to it.

In this book I want to demonstrate to you that you can greatly improve your ability to ask questions and that doing so will benefit your performance and prospects. It will improve your leadership ability, your selling techniques, the way you communicate with customers and colleagues. And it can strengthen relationships with friends and family.

My argument is that good questioning skills will empower you and that they can transform your confidence, ability and results. Why am I so sure of this? Because I have seen it work. As a business consultant and trainer for more than twenty five years I've had the privilege to see things at the coalface of production, in the heat of the boardroom, and in just about every working environment in very diverse organisations. During this time, as a negotiator, trouble-shooter, consultant and trainer I've learned to observe, analyse, reflect and, above all, to ask questions and then listen very carefully. I am humbled by how effective this process can be and I am passionate in my belief that everyone can gain immeasurably by asking better questions.

It would be a marvellous thing if we could all spend our lives asking brilliant questions with the result that these lead to equally brilliant solutions. That is not easy or possible even for the brightest among us. But what we can and I think must do is to continue to exercise our questioning abilities constantly because in that way we will obtain the confidence and ease to ask some very powerful questions sometimes – and perhaps even some brilliant ones. At the same time we will develop a communications tool which is a key we can use to open doors to understanding and to clarity. How

long can any worthwhile business, personal or professional relationship survive without understanding and clarity?

So when we learn to feel at ease asking a few challenging questions
– or when we know how to take our time to ask a customer or
client all about their situation: why do they need us, our products
or services and how can we help them to achieve the best possible
result – that's when we will be valued because we are offering
proper service. In that way we don't just sell something and have
done with it; we make long term relationships, with friends, clients
and customers. Questions can do that.

Or when we, as leaders in business, families or communities, start
to understand that we are not just there to provide ready answers,
instant decisions, solutions and knowledge, but that a big part of
our job is to ask questions – and invite our partners, colleagues and
friends to ask us questions – that's when continuous improvement
becomes a reality and when motivation and morale build up a full
head of steam. One good question can travel all the way through
an organisation shaking up everything in its path – I've seen it
happen and watched the productivity and profits grow.

Only by questioning – and by questioning people in such a way
that they trust us and feel comfortable with the process – will we
truly understand what our customers want, our suppliers need, our
business colleagues feel. By doing this we will achieve clarity, a
sense of purpose, motivation and direction. By doing this we will
also have a vital tool that not only helps us to understand other
people and what their real agendas are, but also to understand
ourselves, where we are going, how much we are achieving and
what we can improve upon. The point is that a big part of the
ability to ask questions well is, of course, to be able to ask ourselves
good questions too. While much of the practical information and
instruction in this book is geared to direct communication within

groups and on a one-to-one basis, the importance of self-review through questioning cannot be overstated. Here are a few reasons why questions are so important:

Questions open doors to ideas and creativity

How many times have you attended a meeting when you have not been engaged with what has been said and when the direction of the meeting has been mostly about providing updates? How much more interesting would the meeting have been if you had been engaged because a good question was asked, perhaps about a system or process or a way of improving an aspect of business? Questions will open doors that often people do not realise are there. They make us think at a different, slightly deeper level and this is an energising and empowering process. In a group situation a question might fetch a poor answer from the first person who responds but this will often trigger a much better answer from the next person who offers a suggestion. Questions encourage creativity and they promote the sharing and exploring of ideas. Otherwise it's just you sitting there and someone else doing all the talking – which is a perfect way to engender a low level of engagement. And the questions asked do not have to be inspired or brilliant. We can all ask something as simple as "What does that mean?" or "What have we missed?" and the ball will always start rolling.

Questions help us to achieve clarity

The speed of business exchanges and general rush to get things done quickly affects us all and often leads to poor outcomes. The reason is that general muddle and lack of mutual understanding will too often lead to poor or ill-thought out decisions. By making it a rule that we question, listen and respond to each other this problem very quickly disappears. Only by questioning our customers, our bosses, our colleagues will we know what they are thinking, what they need, what the purpose of our assignments really are and what direction we need to travel. Lack of clarity leads to crossed-wires, poor collaboration, and the tendency to shelve problems or avoid taking actions, mostly because of uncertainty or confusion about objectives. On the other hand, asking questions will shine a light on purpose and tie energy and action together. Everyone will know what to do, why they are doing it and when to get it done.

Questions act as a catalyst for change and innovation

Some questions are really powerful. They may be as simple as "What are we trying to do with this?" or they may be highly focused such as "How do we ensure that this product is going to sell?" These are the questions that create breakthroughs. They ensure the listener will sit up and take part. They will stimulate reflective discussions and they will focus enquiry and usually evoke more important questions as they lead to changes in the way things are done. Sometimes the outcomes of these questions will be the establishment of entire new organisations within the company, much-needed restructuring, a changed business model or an entirely new product. The process starts with a powerful question that needs to be asked.

Questions empower us

By developing your questioning muscle you will become more engaged in your work, and more in control of the relationships that are important to you. You will have greater self-awareness and an increased sense of purpose and motivation. In effect, improved questioning skills, and better understanding of the value and power of certain types of questions, will empower you. If you, like a great many people, pick up information in all kinds of ways but seldom by asking directly, you will be surprised by how much you will be empowered by developing your questioning ability.

More than this, your empowerment will be self-sustaining and will develop continually if you actively practise questioning skills. You will become more interested and more engaged so that you will think more and develop more clarity about the things you may have taken for granted. Even at the simplest level, you will be more capable of gaining what you want in life or your career.

Questions bring assumptions to the surface

A major source of breakdown in communication occurs where an assumption has been made. In customer relations it happens all the time; we assume that this is what the customer wants – and if they want this they must also want that. It is easy to base our decision about what a customer needs on what we assume he needs, rather than asking just a few questions to check out what is actually required. It's a classic mistake and causes endless frustration and wasted effort. In negotiations making assumptions is also a real danger. Your party might think you know all the facts, have most of the cards on your side of the table and know what the other party's agenda is but you make these assumptions at your peril. You can only check the position in one way and that is by asking. Even an unclear answer, usually combined with body language indicating some tension or discomfort with the subject, will be revealing and will alert you to find out more or to tread warily.

Questions can be impressive

If you ask a good question you will find that this is generally more impressive to your bosses and peer group than the answer you elicit – even if it is a good answer. Asking questions shows you are committed to your work and to business projects and that you actively seek to improve outcomes. And when you ask a good question of a customer or client they will feel you are very much on their case.

Questions can turn negative into positive situations

When you're trying to fix a problem and all you do, figuratively speaking, is stick your joint heads under the basin and jostle for some room to work the spanner, this can be debilitating and pointless. Constant focus on the problem and how to fix it is wearying and it can breed a kind of hopelessness and desire to put the tools down and find something more worthwhile to do. But by turning the focus from what the problem is and how to fix it to what the possibilities are that the situation offers us, we can rapidly convert a negative to a positive outcome. We perhaps need to ask "What's the possibility we see in this situation?" or "Okay, we can't do it that way, so how else can we do it?"

Questions show consideration and interest

By asking questions of others you are demonstrating that you are interested and that you care. Questioning shows consideration and will make your listener feel valued. Quite apart from developing your understanding of a situation, or providing a broader picture, this will build the trust and goodwill in any relationship.

Questions will drive continuous improvement

However good your product or service may be it is an unwritten rule of business success that continuous improvement should be built into the programme. We can always do things better and once we have a product or service just right for the market there are still many external factors to which we must adapt – so we are constantly tuning and hopefully improving our ways of doing things. What happens if we do not pursue a course of continuous improvement? The answer can be applied at different levels. At the level of a business, competitors will get to the market first with better products and services. In the larger scheme of things if people do not try to continuously improve they will not fit into the new world. Careers are changing and industries are changing and they will continue to do so and the rapidity of change means that the next great invention is just round the corner. Through a combination of personal and business goals and through the motivation to improve continuously we are always positioned to adapt to this environment.

Of great importance, a culture of open communication, in which everyone is actively encouraged to ask questions, will strengthen the business' drive to improve continuously. This is a core principle for success. If everyone is told, in effect, to do their jobs and keep their heads down they are not likely to have much interest in the way they are contributing to the business and they are unlikely to think about ways of improving it. In such a business – and they do exist – all the driving has to be done by the leaders. That way of doing things is difficult to sustain. Very often, as the best leaders are fully aware, the greatest knowledge about systems, techniques, particular customers and suppliers, business approaches – and often the greatest talent and skill – lies with other people in the organisation. It is in everyone's interest to channel and pool that wealth of knowledge, skill and experience by encouraging people to ask questions and give feedback.

I am just skimming the surface of a wonderful subject – there is much more to tell you. I am very confident that you will find many other good reasons why skilful questioning can transform lives and businesses.

Over the course of years of business experience I've learned not just how hugely powerful questions can be but also that they come in many and various types. There are probing, challenging, leading, framing, clarifying and many other types of question and they all have their place and distinct value in communication. Once we understand what these types are and how we can use them, we are on the road to empowerment because with this understanding will come proper and better use. There are good and bad ways of asking questions and there are also good and bad times for asking certain types of question. People often carry an inner pocketful of well used 'habit' questions and all too often they do not really listen to the answers given to the questions they ask.

So in this book I'm going to bring some checks and balances into the process. I'm going to demonstrate what makes a good question or a bad question; when to ask different types of question most effectively; and how to ask questions to have the most impact and influence on the course of a conversation, a sales process, or a discussion with a customer or colleague.

There are questions for particular situations just as there are horses for courses but whether you are asking a very simple closed question – one that demands a yes/no answer – or venturing to ask a slightly more inquisitive question, or actually asking a powerful question that could be the catalyst for significant change, the important factor is that you ask.

A major purpose of this book is not just to make you think about good and bad ways of asking questions but to get you asking more questions in more situations so that questioning becomes a thoroughly ingrained habit. When you develop that muscle you are developing a really empowering skill and a highly valuable communications tool.

Like any aspect of communication, the ability to ask questions well is one that we can improve when we understand the range and power of the tool itself. I intend to explain this range and power and provide you with a process for practising and developing your skill in using it, naturally and easily.

Chapter Two

What stops us asking?

The question that may well be forming in your mind at this juncture is "if questions are so effective and powerful why don't most of us spend more of our time and energy on producing them?" There are a number of answers to this and it is worth taking a moment to consider them because this will make us think more about the extent to which questioning skills need to be part of our own communications armoury.

One answer to what stops us thinking about and framing questions concerns the way we operate at a cultural level, in Western Europe and North America. We have developed into a society which demands access to immediate information about a huge variety of subjects – and it is information, not necessarily answers to questions that we seek. The internet is at the core of this information and it has become the first stop for 'ready answers'. But we need to be aware of the difference between a ready answer and the right answer in every circumstance. So at this larger cultural level, as a society, we are generally geared more to obtaining the right answer – in the form of information that is at hand – than thinking about the right question to ask.

The more information proliferates and is readily accessible on the internet, the more embedded this situation becomes. People can check about anything, find facts – and also information masquerading as fact – and learn about specific subjects at the speed of a double click on their computers. Why take the trouble to ask other people when you appear to have instant access to the answers? This is not to say that the internet is not a fantastic reference tool – it most certainly is that – but it is part of a technological revolution which can lead to more passivity, and which arguably weakens our need or desire to engage with others in reflective conversation which involves questions.

Then consider the way children learn from their parents and are educated.

Many very young children are incredibly inquisitive – some of them will ask questions about anything and everything. Parents can often be subjected to what seems like an ear-bashing, high-pitched refrain of Why? Why? Why? Why?

It takes an enormous amount of energy, at a time when one's energies are at a premium looking after young children, to provide good answers to frequent, innocent questions, or at least to take note and to encourage curiosity by providing diverting activities and real attention. The manic questioning tends to be a phase but perhaps it is one that stops too early! Perhaps, exhausted by the barrage of questioning, the answers that parents can be unsatisfactory, dismissive or even hostile. So the torrent of inquisition comes to an end.

When they start school, children quickly learn that questions have a different kind of implication. Suddenly you are supposed to know something and you have to give the right answer – in front of the class. Questions then become associated with risk and danger. You have to revise to be able to answer them in order to pass exams that teachers and parents constantly tell you will be the basis for employer's decisions which in turn will define your place in the world. Ouch and double ouch!

The education system is a massive, highly controversial subject and it is not my domain or the subject of this book. But I do plead the case that if questioning ability is nurtured and fostered from an early stage not only is it more likely that children will be happier and more empowered but they are actually more likely to do well in exams. Why? Because I have seen how productive good questioning ability can be and how it helps us to achieve because, among other things, it promotes curiosity and has the effect of unblocking our memory, thus improving our recall of information. Also, my experience of young people joining the workplace demonstrates that teachers who do encourage their students to ask questions are a credit to their profession. They tend to be the educators who pass on the most learning and really engage their students.

Peer group pressure also has enormous influence on a person's questioning skills, and children and young people can adopt a low profile tending not to ask questions in the company of more gregarious and confident peers – and the pattern tends to repeat in adulthood. Meanwhile, of course, most figures of authority, people who are there to be asked and are usually eager to share ideas or provide guidance, belong to another planet.

So the journey continues from education to the workplace and many young people make this transition without the capability of asking the questions that need to be asked about their roles or purpose – and that will help them to understand the value of contributing to business objectives.

The knock-on effect of this 'missing' ability occurs in every walk of life. I have been in negotiations where people have clearly not understood a phrase or a word and they have come to an inaccurate conclusion about what was meant. Instead of simply asking "what does that mean?" they fail to comprehend. That one missing question is the result of conditioning and experience that I believe goes right back to early childhood and to what people learn – or fail to learn – as they grow up.

The default position for many can therefore be to keep one's head down and simply pick up the information they need to get by – through any means apart from asking direct questions. In a world where we could usefully ask questions, at just about every turn, this would appear to be an odd approach to take. But it is extremely common.

People of all ages are often inhibited from asking questions by a lack of confidence, a sense of vulnerability and downright fear or, if not fear, then timidity. And these factors continue to apply to most of us in various degrees throughout our lives. It is the rare individual who actually dares to ask the question aloud to the person who can provide the answer.

In the workplace, the excuses for not asking can be numerous, for example:

- I don't want to appear stupid
- My boss will think I don't know what I'm doing
- I'm not ready to deal with this situation
- I don't want to challenge the status quo
- I'm afraid of what may happen

There are many other excuses we could add to this list in our responses to different situations. We are highly complex beings and each one of us reacts to things in different ways based on our beliefs, values and life experiences. When we are motivated to learn something or pursue something it is remarkable what we can achieve but when we sense that we might put ourselves in a vulnerable position we can come up with far more reasons for not doing something than for doing it.

We all know from experience that people can be extremely sensitive and sometimes a question that may have a direct bearing on someone else's personal life, behaviour, attitudes, thoughts or feelings is one that needs very careful consideration. The problem is that unless we are in a situation such as in training where we are directly asked to frame questions, or unless some information or fact-finding is exceptionally important in a meeting or interview situation, it remains easier to keep one's own council and not ask.

We should consider the effect of this for a moment.

In negotiations or in situations when we are trying to steer a path through some difficult issues, the meeting room can be full of frustrations, each one representing the bottled feelings and strongly felt emotions of the participants. While any questions in such a circumstance need to be considerately phrased and carefully framed we should still have the courage to ask them. In these situations it is questions that will throw light on the tangles and confusions that lead to these conflicting emotions. And it is only questions that will bring the key issues to the surface for considered discussion and negotiation. Not asking them, as calmly and clearly as possible, is a form of avoidance that will only keep the pressure in the bottles and the gauge in the red zone.

Or looking at this in a more general way, fear and lack of confidence about asking questions can have a massively crippling effect on our performance. Too often we will fall in one or other camp: either we try to rush to get things done quickly and fail to achieve the desired outcome because of lack of preparation or proper consideration, or we hold back and think "I would do this but it's too risky, too frightening. I'm not ready for this." But if we learn the importance of asking questions, checking our own progress and reigning in our emotions, we will have the benefit of calmness, we will achieve clarity and we will operate at a higher level.

Just to illustrate the typically human desire to rush at things and get things done as quickly as possible, when I previously worked in financial services I often said to people in training situations that the most valuable tool they have is their fact find document – which creates understanding of the client's needs and ambitions. The more you understand about your client's or customer's world, what they are trying to achieve, what they care about and what their real interests are, the better you are in a position to help them and make a good sale. Sometimes it is possible to rush to sell products; sales can certainly be achieved this way and the young buck salesperson might think they have a feather in their cap. But rushing to achieve a sale is nowhere near as successful a process as gaining a good understanding and then making a suitable sale. In this way you will have a sure, long-term customer and repeat business. The way to achieve this is to ask questions and to listen carefully – it's the basis of a successful relationship.

Questions can also stimulate really good ideas which will improve performance without necessarily requiring improved ability. One example of this is in a group or team situation when people are considering a particular issue. Let's imagine that the team leader asks a simple but probing question, such as "How can we improve this situation?" The first person to answer that question will not necessarily come up with a great answer, it might even be a poor answer but it will trigger a response in someone else's mind and that person's answer could be just what you are looking for. In that situation, who actually generated the right answer? Was it the person asking the question, or the person daring to put up the first answer or the person coming up with a better answer? It can be argued that it was all three because what this example shows is a journey of continuous improvement starting with the initial question and moving through to a great answer.

Here's another example directly from my experience which shows how transforming a question can be, but this time in a complex situation where people appear to have met a dead end.

I was in a global engineering company, a successful electronics business. A number of people were wrestling with a very serious contractual issue concerning one of their important customers. In effect, the customer was asking them to do something which they felt, for good reasons, was inappropriate.

Seeing there was an impasse, someone asked one simple question: "So you can't do that, but what can you do to help this customer?" And this completely changed the dynamic of the meeting. Some very clever engineers in the room started to look at the problem from a completely different perspective. Asking "what can you do?" literally created a "can do" solution.

Our emotions, perceptions and also our prejudices can all have the effect of preventing us from asking questions or at least they will inhibit our abilities as communicators. This will directly affect our performance in meetings, interviews, sales discussions, customer handling and many other activities.

Consider the situation, for example, where you are about to attend an important interview. This is the point when the nerves set in and you start to doubt your ability to communicate clearly and to describe your experience and skill set properly. But this is a potential problem that not only affects you but also affects your interviewer. I have sat in on numerous interviews where the interviewer has clearly been aware of the impact of his or her questions on a nervous interviewee and is trying, unsuccessfully, to put them at ease. Interviewers then struggle slowly and painfully to pull out the strengths and uncover the weaknesses of the candidates. The problem is they are ill-equipped to do this properly because their questioning abilities are poor.

In interviews good questions are very important for both parties and preparation and practice for all involved is an excellent way of improving the process and the results. For example, for the interviewee a classic question that they could intelligently ask – but rarely do ask – is "What particular qualities are you looking for that will most suit this role?" If you are about to embark on a period of interviews, as interviewee or interviewer, there is a lot to come in this book that will strengthen your hand.

Sometimes people do not ask questions because they do not really want to know the answers. They believe that moving along inconspicuously and getting the job done is enough. Without much embellishment it might appear that I am describing someone with a lack of ambition and possibly with quite low self-esteem. But, ambitious or not, we are probably all at fault for not asking ourselves enough questions, let alone putting our heads above the parapet and asking questions of others . Regular self-review is not only healthy it is extremely useful. How do I feel about this? Can I alter this situation beneficially? What do I want from this employee? Where can I go from here? Am I doing my work well enough? How can I improve what I do? Just asking the question will raise one's head and will set up an internal dialogue that will lead to answers, renewed efforts and the discovery of different ways of doing things.

Questions demand energy but they repay that energy many times over. As we see in the next chapter, this is true right across the spectrum of life and business activity.

Chapter Three

When are good questions most effective?

Once you start improving your questioning skill you will find that this will have a hugely positive effect on all aspects of your personal development. But I would like to anchor down some specific areas where questioning abilities make a remarkable difference and have an empowering effect on your achievements in your career or business, your relationships and life in general.

Bear in mind that this is just an outline, focusing on the positive effect that good questioning skills have within each of these organisational activities and business roles. You will find that the practical instruction in later chapters can be applied beneficially in all these activities and roles – and in others too.

Developing leadership skills

Now you might be thinking that leadership doesn't apply to you. But leadership sits at many different levels. In its basic form the purpose of leadership is to get people to take action to do or achieve something. From this perspective most people are engaged in leadership activities in work, family, hobbies or social lives.

Leadership is all about asking questions: the right questions at the right time in the right way. This process starts from within. In order to be able to lead others you first have to be able to lead yourself. By asking yourself questions that clarify your thoughts you can understand what's affecting you and improve the way you manage your own emotions. Then you are in a position to understand what's happening to other people and how best to direct them.

Essentially leadership is enabling people to take action, preferably with a good heart, in order to achieve results. This process includes consideration of what people need, what they need to see, what they need to feel and what they need to believe. You must understand these factors in order to influence them, to ensure they understand what's expected and to get commitment to the task. You will achieve this best of all by asking questions and encouraging people to ask you questions too.

This skill not only applies in the workplace, it also applies at home, and to every situation where you need someone to do something for you. Give it a try next time you want your partner or children to do something for you and try it when you need to get good customer service from your mobile phone company, or bank.

When someone comes to you with a problem they may expect an immediate solution or decision from you – and your first instinct may be to suggest a solution. But while suggesting a solution might be the quickest way to get something done, the short-term gain is overshadowed by the long-term costs. You can add much more long-term value by asking the right question and helping someone to find their own solution, quite possibly even a better one than you can come up with yourself. I see this all the time in the work I do in improving organisational performance – nobody knows everything or has all the best answers. Not only will you be helping to build confidence and motivation, thus contributing to the individual's development, but you will also find that you are unlocking a source of fresh ideas. Do this across a team and the effect multiplies; it's amazing to see this in operation.

Through questions you can enable people to find a solution even in situations where it seems that there is nothing they can do. By asking can-do, probing questions a solution will be found and action can be taken. In this way, leaders can also reveal training requirements, new innovations and generate better solutions that people can own and want to implement themselves. Ultimately, it is the success of achieving not the leader that motivates people in the long haul, and it is this that keeps them happy in their work.

A considered question can help people to see what they have contributed. I can remember working with the Fire Service on a customer service training project. Part of the process was working together to define skills and standards and I had to interview a whole range of staff to gain insight and understanding. I came away feeling rather embarrassed about how little I knew about what the Fire Service actually do and how they contribute to our safety and well being.

One day I was interviewing two people who help prevent fires through education and training. The passion they demonstrated for their work was deeply impressive and I gained some very valuable ideas from their stories too. Such stories help us to be more aware of how we are influenced by others, how easily we can make mistakes by not being prepared to go against the norm and, in a fire situation, by not getting out of the building immediately. I was so impressed that I shared these stories with other as part of my own training in improving organisational performance. I told the people from the Fire Service what I was doing and their response really surprised me. They didn't react. I was expecting them to say that's great and to be pleased about hearing that their work was spreading through our training and was being used to inspire others. This took me by surprise, so I asked myself: why did they not seem excited or pleased? Maybe they take what they do for granted, as to them it's all part of the job. So I went and asked them. Do you mind if I ask you an off-the-wall question? No, of course, not came the reply. You know when I was telling you about how I have plugged some of your training into mine, you really didn't seem that pleased. Can I ask you – do you take what you do for granted? The reply was a resounding yes.

The reality is everyone needs good feedback, to know that they make a difference. It doesn't hurt to remind those who say they don't need it too. Asking questions reveals what people do, how they contribute, and how they inspire others.

Some of the best leaders that I have observed are quick to ask and slow to answer. There is a terrific leader who I worked with in the Packaging Industry and his approach is to ask members of his team for recommendations; he then offers his ideas on what he feels might work differently and asks again what they feel about that. In this way he builds consensus and shared purpose, and shares information about direction, problem-solving, new ideas and strategy. He certainly does not simply tell people what to do.

Here is another example. I was working with a company that on the surface looked wonderfully organised. The factory was spotlessly clean and had state-of-the-art machinery all lined up and ready to go. The leader also appeared to be saying all the right things. I was asked to go along to a team briefing and clearly this was because the leader wished to demonstrate how the team all sung together in concert. First of all I was really impressed and then someone asked a question. What has happened about this particular contract? The answer was completely negative and really no more than a rebuke: it's not your place to ask that. This question and response was enough to tell me that all was not as well as it seemed, that the business operated a blame culture, that communications were poor, ideas and questions were not encouraged and much more could be done to motivate and engage employees.

Leaders are in a key position to influence and shape the business and to do this they should ask some compelling questions that will engage everyone. For example:

About core values:

- What are our core values?
- What are we passionate about?
- What must be shared by our people?

About core purpose:

- What is our purpose?
- What targets must we achieve?
- What will sustain the growth of our business?

About our vision:

- What is our vision?
- What needs to change in our organisation?
- What do we do first?

Every day a leader is also in a position to create greater value by asking empowering questions. For example:

To achieve clarity:
"Can you explain more about this situation?"

To construct better working relations:
Instead of asking, "Whose fault was that?" ask "what can we learn from this?"

To make people think more critically:
"How will that help you?"

To engage people in the process:
Instead of asking "Here's the task, do you all understand it?" ask "Here's the task; how will you implement that?" and later ask "What have we missed?"

To help people to reflect and see things in a fresh way:
"Why did this work?"

To encourage more breakthrough thinking:
"Can we do it another way?"

To create ownership:
"How do you suggest we do it?"

To elicit feedback:
"From your perspective what should we add to this brief?"

Even if this approach is completely new, I suggest you try it for a few weeks. By doing this people will feel that they are part of the decision-making process and will start to challenge you constructively and share their ideas. When they do this you will realise that you have a motivated and inspired team – and your results as an organisation will improve dramatically.

While the CEO of a global organisation is likely to have a different type of leadership skill, leadership qualities pertain at every level of an organisation and we can all develop them further. Everyone has the power to influence, which is a key ingredient of leadership, but some people decide not to use that power or do not believe they

have the capability to do so. Others lack the con
ence to use their ability to influence. But right
we fill in an application form we can exercise inr
are at an interview we have the choice of being complete,
sive and letting the interviewer steer the entire event, or we
exercise our influence, our leadership in effect, by preparing some
really good questions which will show the level of our thinking and
perhaps give the interviewers some insight into our real capabilities.

Motivating and self-motivating

The difference between a motivated employee, team or indeed
business and one that is simply going through the motions is
phenomenal in terms of productivity, profits and success. One of
any leader's top priorities is to ensure that the team is motivated
and a great contributor to a motivated workforce is the demonstration that you care, you listen, you enquire and you take notice.
Asking questions is central to this approach.

A great deal of a company's success is dependent on the company's
culture and a motivational culture will be one in which all the
workforce feel they are contributing towards a vision to which they
all heartily subscribe. Within each team people also need to have
their own goals, sense of achievement, acknowledgement for good
work and rewards for high performance. However, a motivated
individual is by no means someone who is simply paid well for
good performance. When leaders and managers take note of
particular aspects of an individual's contribution – their own
particular successes in whatever ways these are demonstrated –
this can greatly improve the employee's motivation and help to
sustain a high level of performance.

recognition for work done well is dependent on a good relationship between an employee and those to whom they report. But sometimes top performers do not have others to measure or qualify their own activities to the same extent. A certain amount of self-analysis and the setting and pursuit of one's own targets can help, but it is still useful to be accountable to other people. I have often observed that people will procrastinate and not work to optimum levels when the work they are doing is for their own benefit, whereas the energy is far more evident when they are working for someone else or are part of a highly motivated team. There are various ways round this. We can actually cheat ourselves by imagining we are working for someone else; we can use someone else as a sounding board to qualify and assess what we are doing; or we can directly ask someone else to help us.

As an example of this I occasionally visit a client who is a highly successful entrepreneur and we will have three-hour meetings which primarily involve me listening to his ideas and strategies for the company. During these sessions I will ask a number of questions. Why are you doing that? What will that achieve do you think? How will that improve the situation? And I will listen, taking off my hat as a business adviser and consultant and just acting as a sounding board. He is, in effect, giving rein to his ideas and by airing them intensively and using me as a sounding board he puts some order and priority on his highly creative thinking. What this process achieves for the client is clarity.

To put a different slant on this, there are other ways to achieve our personal goals more quickly. For example, I have set myself a particular goal to be achieved within a given period but I am actually accountable to no one for achieving it. I have therefore arranged for a particular person in Ireland to phone me at the end of that period to ask me whether I have achieved that goal. I will then pay him a sum of money that he will appreciate just for doing this. By making this commitment and by involving the other person I am certainly more motivated to achieve this goal and, God willing, I will do it!

For some people, self-motivation is a major issue and we can achieve and sustain it by changing the way we look at life and the world. Lack of self-motivation usually stems from a negative approach to processing information about ourselves and the world about us – in effect, we answer questions about our own position, achievements and contribution in demotivating ways. We may also get caught into a downward spiral of negative thinking about work-related issues. All these factors can be highly debilitating and will serve to reduce our self-esteem and confidence as well as our motivation to do things well.

In such a mode of thinking, if our boss asks us to do something that we don't want to do it is a natural response to do it reluctantly with the result that it is likely to be done inefficiently. In this way we will sustain a demotivational way of working and will not do as well as we are capable of doing, so that our potential is unrealised.

By using questioning techniques we can actually change the way we look at a task to create a sense of motivation, a sense of purpose and a sense of achievement. It is true for most of us that if we have a task that we just do not want to do and eventually we do it, we feel a sense of relief and achievement. We need to recognise that we should do the difficult things first, or as a matter of priority, to create this relief and achievement. We can motivate ourselves if we ask the following types of question: How will I feel if I get this done? What will I achieve if I do a really good job of this task? How will that help me?

Improving customer service

Questioning techniques sit right at the heart of good customer service.

If you want to please a customer who phones up to complain about something, do your best to find out about the exact circumstances. What is the nature of the problem? Can you explain how the product isn't working or why this service did not work for you? And, most importantly, listen attentively to the answers and show that you are listening by asking more questions and getting as much detail as possible. The more you can find out the more you will be in a position of clarity – you will know, for example, that the customer has clearly not followed instructions or that the installation was done poorly and you will know what programme, what tools, people or approach are necessary to rectify the problem. Slow down and gather all the facts and you will save your company a fortune in the process. And just as valuable as achieving clarity you will make the customer feel pleased that you are enthusiastic about helping them and they will feel properly valued. The result of this is a customer who will remain with you for the long term – and who will recommend you to others.

This being the case, it is surprising that a lack of questioning is common in many customer service situations – whether they are conducted by phone or face-to-face. And those that are conducted by email or letter will sometimes reveal a stunning lack of engagement with the customer's actual problems or issues. Too often customer service staff simply reach for a stock reply that makes all kinds of assumptions about what the actual problem is. When someone feels let down by a product or service, a standardised approach is just the way of turning annoyance to anger.

The reason for this apparent lack of real concern is often the desire to rush and this can be a problem even if this desire is promoted by the wish to find an effective solution quickly in order to please the customer. For example, people may be too quick to send out a service operative, without taking sufficient time to learn enough about the problem so that when the man with the van turns up at the customer's premises he has the right equipment or spare parts with him to do a proper and effective repair.

Questions can also be useful in helping to moderate and calm a situation – particularly important for customer services operators who have to confront very unhappy and even hostile callers. Questions show interest and concern so by listening to customers, understanding their situation and world-view correctly, they will feel valued, begin to calm down and then together you can agree the way forward. It's a fact that asking few questions demonstrates a lack of interest and capability, so ask more, uncover more and add more value to your customer relationships. There is always something you can do to help. When you have reached the agreement as to what will happen next, make sure you have asked all the questions you need to ensure that what you are promising will be achieved. We all use assumptions creatively when we discuss and put forward outline ideas but a good rule is never to make assumptions when dealing directly with specific customer issues.

Developing sales techniques

Good selling is not about telling, it's about asking. Everyone is selling at some time or other, maybe not a product or service, but themselves to gain a job or promotion, or an idea or buy-in to a project. To be successful in sales and to ensure a successful client relationship for the longer term you must master the art of asking questions.

Why?

One of the foremost reasons is in order to acquire information and understanding – and to demonstrate that you understand. A conscientious professional salesperson will put in a good deal of time and trouble to find out about the customer and to learn what they really want. In the same way a doctor will ask a good many questions of his patient in order to have enough information to make an accurate diagnosis.

Another good reason is that the person asking the right questions is usually the one steering the discussion. This form of control can be used gracefully to lead and direct the client to a successful outcome – a solution, sale of a product or service that the customer really wants – and achieved without the customer feeling controlled because they are providing answers about their needs and expectations. Alternatively this control can be abused. Typical abuse is making a sale that is not appropriate for the customer just for the sake of making the commission or target. As a sales professional who is steering the discussion it's your responsibility to serve the client in a proper manner and for this you need the right information.

Selling is a career that is relatively easy to gain entry into and this can be a problem. Too often professional sales people receive a frosty reception, not necessarily because of anything that they have done personally, but because of the ones who have gone before them. But where would we be without sales people? The world would certainly not be a better place. They create change, opportunities for growth and ultimately the job security we all rely on. The best way to make progress is to be interested in how you can help people get what they want and the best way to find that out is by asking questions and listening to the answers – continually.

Another essential part of developing a strong client relationship is to make constant and regular contact. This means you are not just calling the client when you want to sell them something or to ask for a payment. You are contacting them to provide the sense that you are there if they need you. The best way to do this is to have a checklist in which you list all your clients and make a note of all the ways that you contact them – letter, email, phone, lunch, appointments, sports or corporate events – and also how often you make contact. Then use the list to ensure that you can maintain frequent short contacts, which tend to be far more memorable for the client. How often you do this depends on the nature of the product or service you are selling but it is a useful rule to contact everyone on your list at least once a quarter. And when you make contact you need to have some good questions ready to hand which are part of a conversation that is relevant to the client. The goal is to ask questions considerately so as to build a good long-term relationship and learn how the client feels about certain issues. Gradually you will acquire more relevant information and will develop an accurate picture of your client's needs, wants, feelings, sense of humour and personality.

A good way to check your own progress in establishing these relationships is not just by reading the bottom line. Making sales is critically important and having a good flow of return business is a sure sign of success. But you should also question your own approach, your own motivation and values. For example, as you build relationships with others are they able to determine your own beliefs by how you behave? Is your behaviour and approach consistent? How can you improve the way you do things? What can you change – appearance, tone or presentation style so that you can influence more effectively? By doing this regularly you will gear yourself to adapting and improving your approach. This will also strengthen the trust that is such a vital part of the client relationship.

Equally, you need to keep a careful eye on the relationships you have with everyone else who is part of the dynamic of your sales operation. This means sales colleagues, people working in administration, suppliers, and those who become a special source of referrals. In each case you will maintain the best relationship by asking questions because by doing so you take the lead in demonstrating interest and concern in the people who make your work possible and effective.

I can remember witnessing a brilliant salesman say to a very successful and smart entrepreneur – "This is right for you, it's a no brainer." The client's reaction wasn't helpful to the salesman. This phrase would work with many people. But by rushing, the salesman devalued the client with a careless remark. As it happened, the client was a personal friend of mine; he called me after the meeting and said if you ever bring him here again you're fired. We have been friends for 25 years and I hope this continues for a long time to come.

Transforming interviewing abilities

While it might come as a surprise that questions are fundamentally important to a successful career in sales, it is hardly surprising that people who conduct interviews need to be good at asking questions. This is of course true and I would like to underline its importance by offering a few observations on the state-of-the-art of interviewing from my own experience.

Many people who sit in on interviews are not particularly good at interviewing, do not always know what questions to ask, cannot always judge the right tone or inflection, often ask 'habit' questions rather than really thinking about the quality and merits of a particular candidate, or how to make progress and gather information in a particular circumstance. Too few people are, to all appearances, properly trained in interviewing techniques. Interviewing people is not easy and for those involved in searching for the perfect candidate it can be downright difficult – even for people who do have plenty of experience.

At this juncture I am not going to dwell on the detailed, practical aspects of questioning at interviews – for these are all covered in the chapters that follow and they apply in all kinds of question-making circumstances, not just interviews. But as a general suggestion, think of the interview as a journey that you are taking with the candidate. Start by asking simple and straightforward questions and keep them open-ended as far as possible. This means using the interrogatives – what, why, how where, who, which – rather than questions that could be answered with a specific bit of knowledge or a yes/no. Gradually feel your way, all the while developing trust with the candidate so that when you ask a more challenging or probing question, they will not be thrown off balance.

Apart from the construction of the questions themselves – which we come on to later – the following tips might be useful as the basis for a good interview:

- First of all be a good listener and do not interrupt – although you do need to be able to redirect a conversation that looks to be going off track.
- Set out to distinguish between the person who just wants the salary and the one who really wants to contribute to the success of your team and organisation.
- Prepare well – do make sure you review a candidate's paperwork properly before you start. Sometimes it's evident that this hasn't been done and valuable questioning time can be wasted.

- Set the tone by thanking the candidate for coming, introducing yourself and any panel members, explaining the process and being friendly.

- Have a script of questions. This is really important and it will particularly show that you've done your homework as concerns the candidate's background. It will also help you to be consistent and flexible in your approach to all candidates. If you have some prepared, properly thought out questions you will feel much more comfortable. Preparation will give you a route to follow and free your mind to add good questions as the need arises.

- Know what you want. Make sure you know the skill-set required for the appointment otherwise you may not be able to answer the candidate's own questions and you may ask irrelevant questions, which will confuse everyone.

- Manage your time. Use the questions you have prepared to help you do this. Listen to your instincts about the candidate and, if need be, arrange a follow-up interview to get to the facts you need to make a good selection decision.

- Make notes. If you have several candidates it will help if you write down key responses with your observations so that you have something to fall back on when you review the interview.

- Be prepared for candidate questions. You are representing your company or organisation so make sure you know plenty about the company and not just about the particular appointment. Be pleased to answer candidates' questions and actively encourage them to ask; you will learn a great deal more about them if you do.

- To check how you are coming across during the interview and the type pf organisation you are portraying ask yourself, "Will this candidate want to work for me?" Challenging people inappropriately in an interview situation may put good people off working for you; a third party can help you with this process.

- Try to help all candidates to take away a good impression of you and your organisation. It's a small world.

There are certain questions that you should be careful to avoid in any interview – even if you have the best motives for doing so. These include questions that:

- Are over-personal
- Make assumptions
- Imply the answer you want or expect
- Threaten or intimidate
- Are long-winded

In general, listen to your instincts and go in search of the evidence that demonstrates that you have found the right individual. Try to understand your potential employee's values, intentions and competencies. If in doubt don't hire. This is a rule that I wish I had applied on several occasion in my business life.

Underpinning negotiating skills

It's a common misconception that negotiating is all about forging a deal in which the best negotiators win what they want and the other party loses out. In fact, the best negotiations, and those that will sow the seeds of a fruitful relationship or deal for the long term, are based on the process of working together. Of course, the term negotiation covers an enormous range of situations from deal making in the marketplace to seeking a lasting political solution.

But in most business situations, including purchasing goods and services, negotiating contracts, bringing together parties in industrial relations disputes, even conducting complex mergers and takeovers, many of the principles of good negotiating tactics remain the same. Much depends on the perceived strength of your hand.

A useful guiding factor in negotiations is to find out as much as you can about the other party and what you can agree on without losing sight of your own goals. That, at least, is a route that is likely to lead to a successful agreement. Your ability to question skilfully and listen very carefully is centrally important to the success of this type of negotiation.

I have taken part, as a consultant and negotiator, in a great many negotiations over many years and it is what I have learnt at the negotiating table – or reflecting upon what happened there – that has led me to focus so much attention on the art and importance of questions and developing questioning skills. Questioning tech- niques have subsequently grown in importance as a part of my negotiation training courses.

Above all in a negotiation you need to find out what the other party's agenda is - you cannot make assumptions. You may think you have all or most of the 'negotiables' on your side of the table, or you may think you are in the weaker position when in fact the opposite may be true. You need to push to achieve a level of clarity and understanding which you can only do by asking questions, paying very close attention to the responses and then asking further, more detailed questions. You also need to use your questions to maintain calmness and control – your own as well as other people's. The level of feeling, pent-up and sometimes hidden emotions that lie behind some negotiations need to be gently uncovered and understood. If you ask an aggressive or defensive question the whole process can be set back and you are unlikely to achieve the results you seek.

Good questions improve the odds in your favour, they reveal information that you can leverage to your advantage – the real skill is in doing this in a way that respects everyone's needs and positions and avoids any assumptions. Asking yourself questions will help you to prepare your responses. Having considered responses will help you to craft an agreement that people will stick to.

I have seen questions increase the perception of value, make more and better sales, retain talent, raise investment capital, sell businesses, repair damaged relationships, find breakthroughs where people thought there were none possible. I have seen them achieve clarity of thought and purpose and improve intentions and relationships in all types of negotiation.

Improving time management

Time management is a major subject. We all become increasingly aware of just how important it is as we grow older – because time no longer seems to have the limitless possibilities that it had when we were very young. It becomes a challenge in our lives to allocate our time as best we can and to evaluate what we are achieving.

What questions can do is help us to evaluate our satisfaction, our level of achievement, our happiness, our wellbeing and our contribution. This enables us to reflect properly on the way we allocate our time during the working day so that we give the right amount of time to each task. And this principle not only affects our working day but our whole lives, our family time and personal relationships and our ambitions for the future – the things we want to have and the people we want to be. So time allocation – I prefer this term to time management – is absolutely crucial and is the basis of our success.

Questions will help to bring certain values and behaviours to the surface because in order to become more successful at allocating our time effectively we need to know what drives our behaviour. If we become better at questioning what we are doing, how we are doing it, how much effort we are putting into a range of tasks and what the results are, we will actually gain in self-awareness and learn about the pitfalls and possibilities of our own behaviour. A high degree of self-awareness is a very empowering commodity.

There are three types of people – proactive, reactive and inactive – and of these the proactive is nearest the ideal for someone who wants to progress and achieve. But proactivity does have its drawbacks. Proactive people in action are like fountains of energy and activity; they will be pragmatic, thinking on their feet, eager to get things done and will usually have a stimulating effect on the people around them. At the same time they can be liable to rush at the gates, take on too much work or too many different tasks to be effective, will not prioritise workloads and can be poor at delegating. Regularly stopping to review progress and to ask some important questions will not only keep them on track but will put all that wonderful energy in harness. Just a few questions are needed: What am I trying to achieve? What time frame do I have available to do this? Do I need to be doing this? Who else could be doing this task usefully instead of me?

Once again the object is clarity and these questions bring clarity of purpose to the business in hand – they help to create a vision and they underpin the desire to achieve that vision. They truly support our ability to set and achieve goals, through more disciplined thought and action.

When you are busy, it may seem that taking the time to stop, question and review is just not possible. But this time is immeasurably valuable and productive. It has all the potential of transforming your day into something that is significantly more stress-free and workable.

As an illustration of this, I work with a wonderful person who is one of those rare people who, no matter what you might ask him to do he'll try and do it for you. He is helpful in every situation, extremely positive, very intelligent and kind. The consequence of having these great attributes is that he often gets pulled into doing things that he should not be doing and he hasn't time to do all these tasks well. And his offer to help in every instance can actually do more harm than good because by taking on other people's problems they are not solving them for themselves.

Seeing what was happening we provided him with the 'five minute tool' – a tool specifically aimed at helping him to allocate his time better. This simply means never to agree to do anything for anyone until you have reflected on it for five minutes. So he will now understand the person's request and then give himself five minutes to make a decision. Just this short amount of time allows him to review what is required, when it needs to be done and whether or not he can or should take it on. The five minute tool has enabled him to prioritise his tasks and improve his productivity. He has also learned to delegate some tasks to other people and to reflect on recurring problems that can be dealt with appropriately in other ways, such as through the provision of training.

The underlying point in all this is that the more of a master you become in the art of questioning and the more you follow the techniques and practices I shall explain in the following chapters, the greater your chances are of achieving the very best solutions.

Chapter Four

How do we get at the facts we need?

There are many reasons for asking questions. They help you to assert control of the conversation, they demonstrate your engagement and enthusiasm, they generate fresh ideas and different perspectives and they can be impressive. But fact-finding and acquiring useful information are probably the most important reasons.

The ability to use questions to ascertain facts and information – and there is a distinct difference between the two – is enormously beneficial and empowering in every walk of our lives.

As to the essential difference between facts and information, consider the process of making a sale of a product or service to a customer. You might ask for certain facts such as does the customer own or lease a car, are they looking for a particular model, is fuel economy important, what price range are they looking within? The answers that you receive are facts. By comparison, 'information' is a much broader form of instructive material for the professional salesperson because it can encompass a customer's feelings or views about a subject, as well as more expansive descriptions of what is required. For example, in response to the question "What type of car do you drive now?" a customer may fully describe their car and in so doing not only provide you with a sense of what they require, but also what they feel about the car, how important it is to them and what kind of changes you might help them make.

The combination of specific fact and background information will build a picture of what the customer is like and what their underlying agenda is, as much as what he or she really wants or needs.

I have just used a sales-related example but obviously fact-finding is a primary drive in negotiations, interviewing and good leadership among other roles and activities already covered.

Sometimes fact-finding and information gathering is critically important. Sadly we are all aware of instances in social services and health care where it has appeared that too few questions have been asked, by busy professionals – or at least where only a minimum number of fact-based questions have been asked mostly as a box-ticking exercise. The result might be an undiagnosed condition or an overlooked case of serious child abuse. Very often it is the rush to complete the job and meet the target that in such cases has caused highly trained, professional people to neglect asking enough questions to provide a fuller picture.

So how do we use questions to find all the facts and information we need to build a good picture?

First of all, we require a good working knowledge of the nature of the question itself and how it is constructed.

Closed questions and open questions

There are many different types of question and we look at these in some detail in the next chapter but all questions can be divided into two overarching forms: closed or open.

A closed question is one that expects a specific answer, normally a yes or a no. Most closed questions start with a verb such as Are, Will, Does, Can, Would, Could, Is. Examples are:

- Do you have a car?
- Does your dog bite?
- Is your name Alice?
- Will you be going to the party?
- Do you mind if I ask you a question?

You can readily convert a statement or opinion into a closed question just by adding a tag such as 'aren't you', 'don't you', or 'isn't it'; for example, "It's beautiful weather, isn't it?"

A few closed questions do not start with a verb; these include such questions as "What time is it?" or "Which colour do you prefer, red or blue?"

All these closed questions tend to give you facts, they are easy to answer, they are quick to answer and they keep the control of the conversation with the questioner.

Closed questions are useful in the following situations:

- As opening questions in a conversation which make it easy for the other person to answer and which are not intrusive: "It's great weather, isn't it?"
- For questioning about choice: "Do you like this software?"

- For setting up a desired positive or negative frame of mind in the person being asked by using a succession of yes/no questions: "Are you happy with your current supplier?" "Do they give you all that you need?" "Would you like to find a better supplier?"

- For steering a conversation: "Can we talk more about your own preferences?"

- For bringing conversations or discussions to a close: "Do we all agree?" "Does this make sense?"

As the examples show, closed questions can elicit some very basic factual information but they are not always the strongest way of developing the full picture. Used properly they have a place and purpose in communication and can help you to steer a conversation and keep control of it.

Open questions, by comparison, almost always start with a part of speech called the interrogative – literally this refers to the words that we use to interrogate: who, what, how, why, where, which. Occasionally open questions will start with a verb but usually these will have an interrogative clause in them. For example, "Can you explain what you mean when you say you don't think the system works?" Although this is technically a yes/no question the questioner is directly asking for a fuller answer and the question itself carries an interrogative question within it: "What do you mean...etc?"

By comparison to closed questions, open questions generally require the person being asked to provide longer, more thoughtful answers. They are therefore the best means of gaining insights into another person's opinions and feelings about a subject.

Some examples of the useful application of *open questions* include:

- As a follow-on from closed questions to develop a conversation, or to open up someone who is keeping quiet: "So, how do you feel about the work so far?"
- To find out more about a person, their feelings, wants, needs, possible problems and so on: "Why is that so important to you?"
- To probe for further information: "In that case, what would happen if we changed the specification?"
- To develop a friendly rapport by showing concern: "How have you been after your operation?"

So a discussion, business meeting or interview in which you employ a series of well considered open questions balanced by some closed questions is the best way to make enquiries when you are on a fact-finding mission. The closed questions help to start the conversation, change or steer its direction and summarise progress while the open questions stimulate the other person to think and to provide you with more detail and other useful information.

Training in asking questions has become an important part of my courses for leaders, sales people and negotiators. One of the role plays that we do is to pair up trainees and get one to ask questions of the other for five minutes on a subject provided by us – and often chosen completely out of the blue. As a guide we suggest that the questioner aims to take up approximately 20 per cent of the time while the person doing the answering should ideally talk for 80 per cent of the interview. Having conducted lots of these role plays I can faithfully report that the average number of questions asked during these sessions is normally between 25 and 40 in only 5 minutes – this is a lot of questions which means that the ideal balance is not generally achieved.

A common fault is that those doing the questioning tend to use too many closed questions. This allows the person responding to make short and quick answers that will keep the conversation at the starter gates. And if a respondent wants to make life difficult for the person asking the questions all they have to do is answer yes or no to most of the questions asked. Can I ask you what you think about this subject? Answer: yes, followed by pursed lips and a glazed expression. The conversation will go nowhere painfully slowly if this type of questioning continues. The moment questioners start to use good open fact-finding questions, the discussion will move effortlessly to another level and the 20/80 target will not be difficult to achieve.

Some great fact-finding questions

While the actual content of a question is as varied as subject matter itself, I have learned that there are some really useful fact-finding questions which can be adapted to many different situations. Remember the following and they may help you on any fact-finding mission.

- What do you want to achieve?
- What do you value in this?
- When or how long..?
- What else do we need to think about?
- If we could do this ... how would that help you?
- What does that mean?
- How do you feel about..?
- Tell me about that?
- How does that work?
- What will you gain from that?
- How could we improve what we do for you?

- What's most important to you about this?
- Why is that?
- What do you want to achieve?
- Who else do you need to speak to?
- Why do you need to..?
- Why would they not do this?
- Have I missed anything?
- Do we all agree?
- What do I need to make sure that I do?

Understanding different levels of communication

Successful fact-finding – and indeed questioning used for most aspects of business and general communications – depends significantly on understanding the particular level of communication that you have with your customer, colleague, potential job candidates or those sitting on the other side of the negotiating table. There are different levels of communication and the questioning approach you apply at each level will also be different. The process of questions and answers, listening and discussion is like a journey but it is also useful to think of a ladder which, as the journey continues, will take you sometimes a little further up and sometimes down again between the levels.

If you visualise a pyramid then from the top to the bottom, I suggest we place the following levels of communication in descending order:

1 Personal dreams, aims and objectives
2 Trusted information
3 Emotions and feelings
4 Problems, ideas and recommendations

5 Banter, jokes and trivia

6 Gossip and low value information

When customers, suppliers, colleagues and people assembling for negotiations initially meet, the first exchanges are generally to make each other feel comfortable. As you settle down together and perhaps wait for everyone to arrive, the level of communication will tend to move between the first and the second stages at the base of the pyramid. This is quite standard and has its purpose in the process of establishing mutual trust.

Humour and banter is very common at this stage but I would advise that if you have come with a serious objective in mind be very careful to avoid anything but intelligent humour. People are incredibly sensitive and sometimes very unforgiving so that the odd humorous remark about someone's appearance can be extremely dangerous, even if the offence was completely unintentional. Often people will not appear to react to a careless remark or observation but they will note it and pay it back later. In an interview situation a careless remark can also be recalled and noted against the candidate. By contrast, intelligent humour can be very helpful and using it guardedly can be extremely effective in changing a tense moment or negative situation into a positive one.

I have learned to ask myself some questions at this stage of play. Before I use this humour, what kind of impact will it have? How will it reflect on me and what I'm trying to achieve? Rather than being too carefree with humour I try to be more considered – and consideration is a vital part of the whole process of developing one's questioning skills and it is central to good communications.

The useful questions get underway when you start to explore the basic substance of the meeting – this is the 'problems, ideas and recommendations' level. Initially, keep the questions relatively easy but ask enough to get a reasonable summary of the facts. At the level of 'emotions and feelings' the questions you need to ask may become more probing but by now your intention and your general approach during the meeting will have established a reasonable amount of trust. Your purpose at this stage is to find out what the other person or party feels about a situation or a predicament and perhaps how it affects them personally. If you can achieve an understanding of what your customer, interviewee, or other party in this conversation really feels your fact-finding mission is on the road to success. If at any point you feel there is some hesitation or diffidence in the other party it may be useful to step down using easier, perhaps more general questions until you can move back up the scale. Using this approach you will gradually move up the pyramid and approach the goal.

The level I have called 'trusted information' is where you feel you are making real progress. With a potential client in a sales discussion, for example, you will sense that the point of decision about a sale is approaching, or with a customer needing support you would be close to resolving all the issues and have most of the information you need to pursue an agreed course. In a negotiation at this level of communication you will be aware of where the balance of strengths and weaknesses lie, you will be able to ask about important data that may form part of a resolution. And in an interview situation the trusted data stage is where you have achieved a good rapport and feel that the candidate is becoming open to some more challenging questions.

At the top of the pyramid, the 'personal dreams, aims and objectives' level of communication is as the name suggests. This is where you are sharing and discussing all the information, emotional facets of an issue, the objectives, ideas and any critical problems. You are fully aware of what people really want, what they are like and how your possibly different agendas can be harmonised effectively. Arriving at this level will involve a combination of trusted information, priorities, problems, objectives, feelings and real needs.

In a rounded discussion where we use our questioning approach tactfully, gaining increasing permission and trust to find out more as we move up the scale of communication, we need to balance our own objectives closely with an understanding of the other party's needs and feelings. In that way we will reach a peak level of communication and achieve the best result for all concerned. On the other hand, if we only focus on our own objectives and ignore how people feel about them we are unlikely to achieve peak level communication and we will not get the best results.

I have been involved in negotiations which have truly demonstrated how important it is to take broad account of the feelings of both sides. On one occasion we were involved in a very difficult negotiation and the discussions were at a point where if they had failed this could have led to some very expensive and time-consuming litigation. Through consulting, questioning and listening to both parties, one of the factors that we observed was that there was a tremendous amount of goodwill between them, in spite of what had gone wrong in the contract under review. But the situation was critical and ultimately one or other of the parties could lose a lot of money, and jobs were potentially under threat. Mistakes had been made on both sides, but they had a relationship which had lasted many years. Once we realised that this strong element of goodwill existed, we asked both sides the question: what was the most important outcome of this negotiation for them? Both parties answered that they would like to achieve a result that enabled a continued relationship, despite what had gone wrong.

This implicit goal – the desire to remain in a close working relationship – formed an essential basis for the ensuing discussions because we were able to keep drawing both sides back to it when the talks became difficult. By remembering where we were in terms of the level of communication, we could also relax the pace and occasionally switch the focus to more enjoyable aspects of the relationship, such as the good things that had been achieved, and we could then leverage these aspects in order to take the discussions forward.

Ultimately, bringing parties together and empowering them to build on the goodwill they already have will achieve far more than trying to establish culpability and who should compensate whom. So fact-finding, listening and really understanding, at all of these levels, enables us to focus on the information that we can properly leverage to achieve much better outcomes.

By observing and taking part in hundreds of negotiations, board discussions, interviews and other business activities where good communication has been the key to a successful outcome, what has screamed out at me over many years is that the fact-finding stage is overlooked or poorly accomplished in too many cases. I cannot emphasise strongly enough how important it is. Failing to understand a situation and perhaps making assumptions only to learn later that you are wrong is all too common and it leads to breakdowns in contracts, in relationships and in business performance.

One clear example of this was where a client of mine was involved in a very serious legal battle and case law was put forward by our side to support their position. But instead of taking this case law as read, a very smart financial director went through all the relevant sections and asked the question: what happened when the initial case went to appeal? As it turned out the initial case went in our favour but it had been overturned at the appeal stage. So a really excellent question had been asked at the right time. On the face of it assumptions were being made. However, as it turned out other information was uncovered as part of this fact-finding journey which actually enabled us to win our case. And it was all down to the financial director asking the question about the appeal.

Another hugely important part of the fact-finding process is to develop the picture gradually and surely, double-checking and improving the resolution as you go. It is a human tendency to be impatient and to want to have the answers to everything immediately, to put plans into action and to move on. In the course of really productive communications where you are asking good questions, the picture will unfold gradually, perhaps with the occasional stepping off points where some particularly interesting information is uncovered. As in any design process you start with something useful as a basic prototype, you show it and take in comments and then you improve it. The improvement process will take it through good to excellent to outstanding. So it is with really useful fact-finding – go steadily and surely, engage trust and move forward. This approach enables the proper management of each other's expectations and obtains the best possible results.

Chapter Five

What types of question?

The more you know about the different types of question and the level of communication you need to be at, the more confident you will be about asking a good question at the most appropriate time. So in this chapter we are going to look at the meaning and purpose of different types of question, what their intentions are and what impact they are likely to have on the person you are questioning.

The following list is not an exhaustive one but it covers broad ground and knowing how these questions can work for you will have an empowering effect.

- Scene-setting questions
- Probing questions
- Pace-setting questions
- Clarifying questions
- Challenging questions
- Hypothetical questions
- Framing questions
- Leading questions

- Defensive questions
- Critical-incidence questions
- Consequential questions
- Goal-setting questions
- Closing questions

Scene-setting questions

As the name suggests, scene-setting questions are those that start the ball rolling, open the conversation or set it on track. They are usually exploratory in nature and they help both parties in a discussion to set out their individual stalls and find points of reference.

They should almost always be open rather than closed questions and examples include:

- Is there anything that you would like to ask me before we begin?
- Is this the first time that you have bought from us?
- How can we help you?
- What is the problem?
- What would you like me to show you?
- What would you like to discuss?

In a typical sales or customer service situation, initial scene-setting questions would normally be followed by a short series of closed questions to ascertain some key facts such as name, address, contact details.

More scene-setting questions are likely to follow in most communications – for example, When did this happen? Were you the only one in the car? – so that the broad initial picture starts to become clear.

Scene-setting questions are very important because what you ask and the way you ask it will have an immediate effect on the other party. If you are dealing with an existing customer, engaging a new prospect, establishing the lie of the land at the start of a negotiation, beginning a performance appraisal – among countless situations – you will be seeking to show openness, calmness and goodwill. These questions set the tone of the communication and are likely to have a big influence on everything that follows.

For example: a manager about to do an appraisal looks up and says to hard-working but nervous young appraisee, 'What kind of tie do you call that?' as an opener; he means well but his dry humour might be misunderstood. A better question would be 'You look very smart today; is that tie new?'

Or a lady walks into car dealership reception having been searching for a while for someone to talk to about a new car. Eventually she finds a salesperson who says 'Are you looking to buy the car today?' which is more annoying than useful. A better question would be 'Have you seen a car that you like?'

A smile and a good degree of respect and appreciation will go a long way to help you get things moving in the right direction. And, whatever the response, don't forget to listen.

Probing questions

A probing question is one that is used to drill down a bit further to find out more information. In a sales or customer servicing situation this is when you are trying to uncover the real issues, problems, needs or wants that matter most to the customer.

Probing questions are intended to help the person being questioned to think more deeply about the issue at hand. For example, when we are trying to solve problems we would use a probing question to drill down further. At the same time we would use it to shift the level of communication to a point where the best solutions are most likely to be found. In doing so we need to be careful not to imply or apportion blame. Probing questions also empower people who have a dilemma to solve their own problem rather than deferring to someone else.

Examples of probing questions include:

* Why do you think that is the case?
* What would have to change in order for..?
* What do you feel is right in this situation?
* What's another way you might ... ?
* What would it look like if..?
* What do you think would happen if ... ?
* When have you experienced something like this before?
* What was your intention when ... ?

Probing questions are widely useful; they are usually brief to ask and they tend to elicit a slow response because they require more thought as they move responses from reaction to reflection. In any form of conversation they require a certain amount of trust to have been established before they are asked.

The power of a probing question is in its ability to broaden the discussion and to gather more information. The question will usually act as a catalyst and will stimulate people's memories and their ability to add detail to a developing picture. In negotiations, for example, I have noticed there is quite often a failure on the part of negotiators to recognise that what they actually have as a point of leverage is what is actually on the other side's mind – rather than what they perceive to be on the other side's mind. A good probing question will bring out so much more and we will learn what people feel, what they are really thinking and what their interests are. All of this substantially adds to our ability to achieve a successful outcome.

When dealing with customers, failure to ask probing questions can mean that you do not find the root of a problem or grievance, or the solution you propose is made too hastily to be effective. In an interview, failure to ask probing questions is too often the reason why companies take on a candidate and find out three weeks later that this was not the person that they thought they had hired.

The impact of a probing question is normally very positive because a customer, colleague or candidate will feel that the questioner is truly interested in finding out more about their agenda, feelings and needs.

Pace-setting questions

As the name might suggest, a pace-setting question is one that has the intention of obtaining quick results or moving the conversation quickly on to the next stage. This type of question is important to understand but is best avoided because it is normally pushy by implication and will not have a positive effect on the person being questioned.

Examples of pace-setting questions include:

- Are we there yet?
- Will it work this time?
- What else can you give us?
- How did that happen?
- Will you sign for it now?

Much depends on the way the question is asked and when it is asked. This type of question may have its place at the closing stages of a negotiation or sales approach at the higher levels of communications discussed earlier – where all aspects of communication are good, priorities have been clarified, problems discussed and a solution is commonly agreed. If you need an answer to this sort of question first of all ask yourself "If I were to be asked this pace-setting question at this juncture, what would I feel about that?" Then you are more likely to gauge whether such a question is worth asking. In most situations, pace-setting questions have a negative impact on the person being questioned.

Clarifying questions

A clarifying question is used to find out more but, as against a probing question, the intention is to achieve a fuller understanding about a circumstance, piece of information or a situation, so that both parties have the same understanding. In an interview, you might use a clarifying question as a way of helping fellow panellists to understand more about a subject that a candidate has mentioned which is your area of expertise and not necessarily theirs. It is important to distinguish between a clarifying and a probing question. In the former you are establishing the facts and the response will normally be quick and reactive in nature rather than reflective.

Examples of clarifying questions include:

- Which of the issues is most pressing?
- When you do this, what happens?
- When we arrive, who should we ask for?
- You say you prefer blue, which shade of blue would you like?
- Have you got everyone you need on board to make this happen?

Essentially therefore, clarifying questions look for the nuts and bolts of a situation, the important additional details that help to sharpen the focus on a particular subject. They are suitable to use at any stage of a communication. When dealing with customers, your boss or even a future employer they show that you are being attentive and that you are interested in their situation, needs and wants. In general they have a highly positive impact.

Challenging questions

There are various degrees of challenging questions and all of them have the effect of putting the respondent on the spot and making them think. Because they can come as a surprise and not always a pleasant one, this type of question can be on the borderline of intimidation, which is to be avoided in most situations. The intention of a challenging question is usually to find an alternative, to change a perspective or even to create a great focus on the real issues.

Challenging questions are potentially the most valuable questions because, asked at the right time and given a high degree of trust in the relationship, they can create the best thinking. If the respondent does not feel safe, or confident in their abilities the response is likely to be negative.

Some examples of challenging questions include:

- What have you learnt from that situation?
- How did that make you feel?
- What skills do you need to improve upon to get that role?
- Is this the only idea you have?
- Why should we do this?
- How would you describe yourself in one word?

In interviews, challenging questions certainly have a place although it may not be useful to start at the very beginning with a challenging question unless you are interviewing someone in whom you require very particular talents. You must also be wary of hiring someone on the basis of impressing you with their answers to a number of challenging questions only to find that the individual actually needs to be challenged all the time in order to work effectively. In other words the challenge acts as a form of support mechanism.

Generally, challenging questions should not be asked without the permission of the respondent – they should come at a stage of the conversation or interview when trust has been established. They are not usually suitable in customer servicing situations. Good challenging questions; for example, when a team leader is trying to generate new ideas from his team members, can open people up to some very creative thinking; bad ones can simply put people off. It is important to watch out for the borderline between challenging and intimidating questions; the latter, in the form of questions such as "How could this have happened?" or "Who is responsible for this?" will shut off creative thinking and make people think they are being judged or blamed.

Hypothetical questions

A hypothetical question is one that is based on a theoretical scenario – that is, one that is not yet reality but which is plausible. The intention behind a hypothetical question is to see how a person would respond in a situation that may or may not really concern the subject in hand but which could throw light on the person's aptitude, feelings or viewpoint. In negotiations, selling or situations where you are trying to influence, a hypothetical question are a useful way of finding out things that would not be easy to elicit from more direct questions.

Some examples of hypothetical questions include:

- When you are solving a problem for a customer and it seems that you have exhausted all options, what would you do?
- Supposing the component was delivered a week late, what would you do then?
- If you were in my shoes, what would you do?
- How would you cope if you needed to relocate?
- What would happen if we cut over-time pay to basic rate?

Hypothetical questions can be used effectively to bring focus to a discussion and to gain agreement. Like probing questions they are certainly not to be used too early in a discussion, because they assume a certain level of communication has already been achieved and they usually concern new ways of approaching detail. At the same time they are not intended to be overly challenging and they should generally be easy for respondents to answer. Sometimes they can be used as humorous interjections to lighten a conversation and generate a relaxed atmosphere.

Usually hypothetical questions have a very positive impact on the respondent. They can be used to gain instinctive answers to difficult questions. When used carefully it's almost as if they fly beneath the defensive radar that we all possess.

Framing questions

Framing questions help people to visualise a situation, literally putting them in the picture, so that they can share the answer with you easily. People usually think in visual images and the framing question can assist the direction and focus of a conversation by building on this tendency. The intention of the framing question is therefore to enable the customer or respondent to relate more directly to the context or meaning behind the question.

Some examples of framing questions include:

- If we invest in this new equipment, what will we need to do to the layout of the factory?
- Where will you go on holiday in your new car?
- What will it feel like to achieve those results?
- How will you gain buy-in from your team?
- To achieve those results how many new people will you need to hire?
- Who will you celebrate your success with?

Putting the question in the picture frame is a great way of making people comfortable with the process and of finding out what really matters to them. Framing questions are, therefore, very useful in the fact-finding stages of a discussion and also for presenting information about a subject. They can additionally be used to lighten a mood or moderate the tone of communications as a means of continuing the discussion after a series of probing or even challenging questions.

Leading questions

There are two types of leading question. I would like to endorse and the other I would dismiss.

One is where the answer is implicit in the question so that the questioner is actually imposing a view, opinion or statement directly on to the person being questioned. For example "You don't like working in this department, do you?", "You were there, weren't you?" or "Don't you agree that the problem here is lack of training?" By its very nature, this sort of leading question will not help you to dig out much information and it is aggressive in style rather than friendly or sympathetic. It is often used in an interrogation where the questioner is seeking to browbeat the person being interviewed into making admissions. But, however it is used, this type of leading question will normally have a negative impact, it will often evoke a defensive reply or make people retreat from the conversation or discussion. It is best avoided.

Over years of looking at question types more closely and training negotiators and others in the art of questioning, I have adopted a different type of leading question and one which has a far more positive impact.

This version is a question which can be used for fact-finding and for gaining commitment and also for taking the discussion on to the next stage.

Examples of this type of leading question are:

- If we adopt your approach, how might this affect the team structure?
- When you chose this company, what factors attracted you?
- Would you be interested if we offered you more responsibility?
- How do you think we can make this offer more compelling for you?
- Now we agree on the principles, what else do we need to consider?

You may be thinking that these are similar to framing questions and you are quite right. The subtle difference is that the frame is set wider and leading questions tend to have a confident sense of purpose and commitment. These questions are very useful for directing the conversation, moving the subject towards a conclusion, to another level of communication, or towards a subject area where the best data or information can be gained.

In my experience the impact of leading questions is highly positive on those being questioned in a negotiation, interview or customer servicing situation. They have great application for leaders and managers when discussing current programmes and forthcoming projects because they stimulate team members to think about particular aspects and allow a rounded, creative or detailed response.

Defensive questions

These are worth remembering if only to be sure not to employ them. Sometimes you might use a defensive question as a knee-jerk response to an objection or criticism. Almost always the effect is negative because a defensive question is a way of battening down the hatches, effectively telling people you do not want to go in a particular direction or that they have pushed too far.

Examples of defensive questions include:

- What do you need to know that for?
- Why do you ask that?
- What else did you expect me to do?
- Who told you about that?
- How is that my fault?

If such a question should even rise to the surface of your mind you know it is probably best to try another tactic, remain calm and think carefully about your next response in order to move the discussion to a happier footing.

Critical incidence questions

Critical incidence questions are a highly useful way of drilling for information and finding out about particular areas of skill, interest or activity in order to build a picture of your customer's requirements or interviewee's abilities. The intention behind them is mostly to make your respondent focus on their achievements, successes (and failures) to illustrate the fact-finding stage of a discussion.

Examples of critical incidence questions include:

- In your current job what was the project that you feel you contributed the most towards?
- Can you give me an example of something you're most proud of from your time at university?
- What did the people in your team ask you for advice about most often?
- What was the most telling sign that our service wasn't working for you?
- When, would you say, was the most productive period of this contract?

Critical incidence questions are usually the reserve of a mid-discussion point, when trust is established and a number of general subjects are coming into focus. Because it is so particular in its intent, this type of question can be very powerful and will often take you right to the core of a subject. In interviews the critical incidence question allows candidates to give rein to what they consider to be their best achievements and it also allows interviewers to make a judgement about how honest the candidates are – and perhaps how self-aware – about their weaknesses or failures. Critical incidence questions play a very useful role in negotiations too because they enable negotiators to require the other party to respond in detail about particular points or areas of a discussion. They can be used in customer service discussions to focus on the specifics of a service or a product that may need addressing; and this makes them great fact-finding tools. They can also help leaders and managers to get team members thinking about their own strengths and weaknesses – particularly useful for performance appraisals.

Critical incidence questions can be usefully prepared in advance and reserved for the right moment. However, once you are fully aware of the construction and intention of this type of question, there will come points in a discussion or interview where an impromptu critical incidence question will spring usefully to mind.

Consequential questions

The intention behind consequential questions is to help people to work out the implications of a situation, and this can be extremely empowering because it enables people to consider particular dangers and risks as well as potential rewards.

Examples of consequential questions include:

* What's going to happen if we don't deliver on time?
* If we lose that customer, what effect will it have on the business?
* By changing the marketing strategy, how will that affect your budget?
* What will you do if we arrive late?
* If we arrange to pick the old one up, what do you want us to do about the new one?
* What have you planned if you don't achieve the target?

Another important aspect of the consequential question is that it enables people to take ownership of a task or situation. Whereas a critical incidence question tends to have the sense of review – looking backwards and making an assessment – the consequential question is all about forward planning. It is very useful for making people think directly about the consequences of their plans or actions and building in contingencies. Another typical use of the consequential question is that when it is self-applied it can be motivational. "What's in it for me if I do this?" "What's going to happen if I keep the Monday morning blues going all day long?" or "How's it going to help me if I do a really good job?"

Target-setting questions

Target-setting questions can be used individually or corporately in any situation and they are particularly useful for enabling, clarifying expectations and gaining commitment.

Examples of target-setting questions include:

- What margin do we need to achieve break-even?
- How many can you complete today?
- How much profit will you make this year?
- When are we likely to achieve critical mass?
- How soon can we get approval from the board?
- Where do you see yourself going after mastering this job?

The great value of a target-setting question is that it focuses thinking on organisational strategy and objectives. It is a form of question that is also useful for interviewers to explore a candidate's feelings and thoughts about his or her own goals and targets for the future. Sometimes it will be a useful way of ascertaining a candidate's perceived degree of ambition, drive and initiative.

Building a high performing team is all about the right people, doing the right things at the right time. The right questions will help you achieve this.

Targets should be SMART (specific, measurable / motivational, agreed, realistic and time-bound). For me there is also another important criteria about setting good targets, and that is the buy-in, the motivation that's needed to achieve them. If your gut instinct is telling you that something's wrong, then it's time to ask questions. Fact-finding questions to remove your reservations.

Closing questions

As the name suggests the intention of a closing question is to bring a meeting, interview or other engagement to an appropriate close. However, it is also very useful as a means of asserting control in a communication, moving on to another stage or gaining commitment to actions, progress achieved and to a sale. In most instances, closing questions happen to be of the closed rather than open type.

Some examples of closing questions include:

- Which option do you prefer?
- Can we proceed with this?
- Does it make sense?
- Will this fit the requirement?
- Is there anything else we need to consider?

In any communication it is important that the questioner uses these types of question intuitively when he or she has reason to believe that consensus is achieved and it is time to move on and conclude the discussion. Applying a closing question too soon will appear pushy or over authoritative and nothing is more likely to put off a potential client or upset a customer who feels that their own situation has not been properly dealt with.

Closing is a vital part of any business activity, because failing to close can mean:

- Wasted effort and expense

- Losing out to a competitor
- A failure to take the action that's needed

A good close is all about helping to make a good decision. Actually making a decision is a problem for some people and there's always a good reason why. Questions will help you uncover and resolve this.

You might find it interesting to see whether you can categorise your own questions – perhaps you will come up with a question that cannot be so easily labelled. There are certainly plenty of questions that cross over to some extent from one bracket to another. I would like to make some brief suggestions as to how you might use the information in this chapter to your best advantage.

Firstly, you will note that I have made repeated mention of intention and impact when I describe the different question types. Intention and impact are two of a number of attributes of questioning that are important to take into account and these are covered in more detail in Chapter 7.

Secondly, just by having an understanding of a reasonably broad range of questions and what their impacts and intentions are, your awareness of the questioning process itself becomes stronger. Some questions are, or can be, complicated in their construction or very sensitive in their use. They sit right at the heart of truly effective communication between people – the point where the two sides of the debate are building knowledge and understanding, exploring key issues and seeking a resolution together. This is why they have so much meaning and effect for me – because they enable people to work together and achieve better things.

The third observation concerns practical application. What do you do with this list of questions? How can you apply them most effectively in your own situation?

Actually, you are already on that road by reading this far, but by doing a little homework you can strengthen your capabilities. For example, you could memorise these types of question and what their impacts and intentions are. You might usefully make your own notes and develop your own thoughts about them and you will find that the message begins to stick and be applied. A useful practice for following this through is to jot down the question type headings on a piece of paper and slip it among your notes in preparation for an interview or particular meeting. Just a glance at 'closing questions' or 'probing questions' might remind you of one or two useful pointers. Remember also the points made about levels of communication in Chapter 4 and conscious questioning practice will become a natural and increasingly easy process.

My belief is practice makes for improvement and there are no short cuts.

Finally, at this stage you may already have been provoked to think generally about examples of your own and other people's questioning skills. I've referred before to people's 'habit' questions which can fall into any of the above categories; you may recall people who have habit questions and perhaps think about your own. I would then question or review the value, intent and effect of these questions and possibly change them so that you can flexibly apply your influence in more situations to achieve greater effect.

Inevitably, there is much to learn, but your ability to question well is a life skill not a four-year degree course so the learning and applying stage depends on what you want to do, how you want to come across, where you want to be, and so much else besides. We teach ourselves and each other constantly if we both question and listen in the right way.

As we see in the next chapter, there are ways of doing this badly that we should avoid and there are ways of doing it well, with extremely beneficial effect.

Chapter Six

What's the best way to ask?

There is a technique that I am confident will improve anyone's ability to ask questions. I've learned it; I continue to develop it and I've applied it in a great many situations. We will come to this shortly.

Firstly, let's look at some important basic principles about how to ask questions well – how to make them really work for you.

The number one rule when asking a question is to be interested in the answer. Good communication both creates and demands a certain amount of energy and your interest in someone else's problems, situation, needs, issues, previous experience – or in finding the solution to a more general question – will definitely create energy. People will respond to this and if you show interest in receiving a full explanation to your question it is most likely that your interest will be rewarded.

It would be difficult to go through life – to conduct every interview, every negotiation or talk to customers in all situations – with your eyes shining with vitality and your face glowing with anticipation. In the fifth, hour-long interview of the day you may just notice that the enthusiastic spring in your voice, if not in your step, is not as it was when you started out. If there are questions in your 'script' or on your prepared list that you are bound to repeat you are likely to ask them, eventually, with less interest than you have before. I emphasise this because it is something we all need to be aware of.

Sometimes, like actors in the theatre, we need to learn how to make our words appear fresh, as if the idea has only just popped into our heads. So keep the energy in your voice, make good eye contact with your respondent, do all you can to show interest and the effort will repay you well, time and time again.

Another important basic principle concerns the way you position a question. We have already looked at a number of different types of question and how some can be used at the start of a communication while others, such as probing, leading and challenging questions, require a certain degree of trust – the permission, in effect, of the person being asked – before you ask them. Your awareness of the place of the question, and also the level of the communication that you have achieved in the discussion, is part of the positioning process. But it is equally important that, whatever the type of question you are asking, you should consider what the impact of the question you are about to ask is likely to be. If we are disrespectful in the way we position a question we are more than likely to receive an answer that is a negative, incomplete or even hostile. Or if we appear to be too obviously leading in the way we position the question, so that we are presupposing the answer or overtly steering the course of the conversation towards our specific agenda, we are also unlikely to get a productive answer.

Remember the idea of the journey and the notion of controlling the conversation gracefully so that you are constantly considering the needs and perceived agenda of the other party. If, in this way, you take your audience on a journey, you will find that the questions almost position themselves. Much depends on the level of challenge of the negotiation, interview, sales process or other communication but if you consider the challenge and start small by asking easy and comfortable questions, you can gradually build on solid foundations making the questions more probing, and you will successfully gain more detail as you progress.

Above all, having expressed your question in a way that demonstrates that you are really interested in what you are about to hear, and having positioned the question correctly, you must then listen to the answer. I have been truly dumbfounded by occasions when interviewers have asked a perfectly reasonable question and then have shown all the signs of settling down for a good nap the moment the respondent opens his or her mouth. Equally, I have been astonished by interviewers who fidget or look distracted, as if they've suddenly remembered that they forgot to turn the gas off, or agitated in a way that suggests they would really like the respondent to get a move on or talk about something completely different. How unbelievably off-putting must this be for a candidate eager to tell you all about themselves and their capabilities?

Listening requires a certain amount of stillness and engagement. You do not have to stare deeply and solemnly into the eyes of the interviewee – this can be off-putting too – but proper eye contact helps and a degree of stillness shows that you are being attentive. The point here is that you must not only truly listen to the answer. By demonstrating to the other party that you are listening you will also develop trust and gain the best answers.

At this point I would like to share with you a very powerful technique for questioning which works in all situations and at all levels of ability and experience.

The QLS technique

We call this the QLS technique, which stands for Question, Listen, Silence. It is as simple as: you ask a question, you listen to the answer and then you remain silent – just for a while. Your silence will encourage people to speak and you will find this very productive; and it works in every situation. In an interview or consultation or even in a presentation, silence can be incredibly powerful. In a presentation, for example, when you are delivering a monologue, you will strengthen it considerably and make people sit up and listen if you punctuate the discourse with silence. It allows people to take on board what has been said and, importantly, it generates a sense of anticipation and expectation, which encourages productive communication.

In a situation where you are questioning someone, the QLS technique creates a discipline which focuses your attention and that of your audience on the question. It enables you to listen for longer and by doing this you will very often find that the other person will use the opportunity to share a little more information, to add detail, to qualify in an enlightening way. Your silence also creates that extra few seconds of thinking time for you to prepare a better response to what has been said or to sharpen the next question that you bring to the discussion.

Our natural desire, as highly social beings, is to keep talking, to keep going at all costs and fill out every gap. We may feel we must make the most assuring noises and be the one doing the questioning or providing all the answers . In such a mode we will have a tendency to weaken our thinking or bore our respondents to death. We might also betray a lack of confidence. By consciously introducing silence into the conversation we avoid all of this. Everyone has the opportunity to take part and has room to listen and share, and there is more focus on the subject and usually more clarity in the way the interaction develops and is explored.

Silence works in different ways according to each situation. In a sales situation, for example, adding silence can create a moment of useful direction. Too much silence is not a good thing because this can result in the customer feeling under too much pressure to buy, but by introducing just enough silence you are actually enabling the customer to think more clearly in their own choice and decision-making process. In training situations I have had feedback from sales people suggesting that if they were to apply this technique and give customers time to think then they might change their minds. My response is that if they change their mind it is a good thing because a customer who changes their mind as a result of a short pause in the proceedings is most likely to have been sold the wrong thing in the first place and would probably pull out of the deal at the first possible opportunity further down the line. By contrast, if you have taken the customer on a journey and truly understood what they need and have listened to them, and then have designed the solution or made a recommendation which genuinely meets their requirements, they will not change their mind. In that situation the silence serves both your interests; it remains part of the engagement process and shows your consideration. You are far more likely to develop a long-term relationship and repeat business with this customer. This is infinitely preferable to a one-off purchase that may well be returned the next day.

The same applies in relationships between partners, husbands and wives, business colleagues and shareholders, where disputes often evolve simply through a failure to just stop and listen.

A classic example of this is a situation in which there were two business partners who had developed a very successful company. They were self-made and had started at grass roots level and they had done very well. But ultimately the business failed and I remember one of the business partners saying to me that if he wanted to he could have stopped this from happening but he just did not want to. The other partner wanted the business to continue and to thrive.

This would, of course, have been possible if only the two partners had communicated properly with each other about their very apparent differences earlier on. In fact, the partners had been offered a sum of money to sell the business which had seemed to be a low price for such a thriving concern but I had asked them the question: "It may be a low price but what might be good about selling the business now? What would this enable you both to do?" They chose to keep the business and, unfortunately, within two years it went bankrupt and they were left with absolutely nothing – the business went from making substantial profits to making substantial losses in just this brief time.

The fact was that they had lost the ability to talk about the things that were important and vital for the success of the business. Either through direct or indirect experience we all know how damaging such a situation can be, especially when it applies to the often more complex dynamic of a personal relationship in a marriage or partnership. The QLS technique has worked for me in all kinds of situations.

At one time I was involved in a very complex negotiation. Some products had been supplied to a customer through a third party; the customer had paid the third party for the products and the manufacturer was not paid by the third party. Then the third party had gone bankrupt owing vast sums of money. The manufacturer came to me to help win back some of the money owed, which I agreed to do on a no-win, no-fee basis. We managed to negotiate a payment of over 75 per cent of the amount owing. This was achieved by following a very clear negotiation process and it is a particular example of the QLS technique at work. There was a stage in the negotiations where the other side, led by one of the most professional negotiators I have ever met – very skilled and astute – agreed that they would pay us some money and had asked for a few weeks to calculate the amount that they would pay. Then we rejoined negotiations to discuss the amount. Initially, there was a very positive atmosphere at the meeting. Then the other side said they had worked out the amount that they were willing to pay and stated what this sum was. It was a very small amount indeed and totally unsatisfactory, much less than we thought would be on offer and certainly much less than we would accept. At the time I was very calm, even laughing inwardly because I knew that there would have been a time when my response would have been typical of many people's response in such a situation, to become cross and aggressive and make a speech about being insulted by such a proposal after so much painstaking work to come to a satisfactory and fair agreement. But actually I felt very clear and calm in my thinking because I had a process to follow and I was now going to apply that process. This takes all the pressure off and allows you to think much more clearly. I used the QLS technique.

The question we asked was simply "How did you come up with that number?" We duly listened to the other side's reply and then remained silent. Listening enabled us to take on board what the other side were trying to say and the silence had the effect of drawing the other side to add more. In particular, the silence promoted them to say that they would also like to offer another amount of money for another part of the contract. Once this was said and we had heard them out and asked a question about how they had come up with that figure. We heard them out and once again remained silent following their explanation. In this way the other side continued to add to their original offer, stimulated each time by the very pregnant pauses that followed questions and explanations.

It was quite clear with hindsight that the other side had purposeful-ly started at a very low figure. But if we had reacted in an aggressive way, we would in all probability have achieved nothing. However, by using good manners, some respect and by asking intelligent questions the offer grew substantially by the end of the process.

How often do I make use of QLS? Well the answer has to be all the time in all aspects of my consulting work, training and business. And I also use it with my family with the direct result that I have greatly improved the relationship with my nine year-old boy because I listen and I allow silence. In this simple way I have created proper, valuable time to take on board what his interests are and what he wants to do.

Another heart-warming example involves the daughter of one of my clients who runs a very successful manufacturing business. He was sufficiently impressed with the QLS technique to decide to teach it to his eight year-old daughter. He reported back to me that, having been an eager student, Samantha was applying rigor-ous QLS on her father, when suddenly she burst out laughing. "Why are you laughing?" he asked. "Because you just keep telling me loads of things ," she replied.

I've used the technique frequently in interviews where the silence allows the interviewees time to reflect on the answers they have just given. The amount of silence that I allow depends on the level of challenge of the interview, and the level of communication achieved, but in most cases I find that the interviewee will add to or qualify the answer they have just given, throwing new light or additional information to the answers already provided.

I should qualify this by adding that silence clearly can be intimidat-ing and make people feel nervous. In an interview situation so much depends on the positioning of the questions you ask and the way you take the interviewee on a journey with you. If you move into the level of communication where you can ask particularly challenging questions – for example where you suggest a particular work scenario and you are asking the interviewee what he or she would do in a situation like that – then you will have tacitly built the trust and gained the permission to apply a very healthy length of silence following the answer.

Without doubt the QLS approach is very powerful indeed, it enables you to get to grips with what people are saying and gives them the opportunity to give a better account of themselves.

QLS can be used for all kinds of problem-solving and because it is a vehicle for openness, exchange and participation and it can achieve this without apportioning blame, which is incredibly empowering. Therefore QLS has great effect in performance appraisals, dealing with performance issues, handling disputes, staff problems – in so many situations where there may be unreleased tension, where something of a blame culture is at work, or where staff have wedged themselves into a hole by adopting a victim mentality. By using questions to help people to work out what the issues, problems and options are, by listening carefully and then introducing silence, you will transform your ability to achieve solutions. The process can genuinely save a fortune in legal fees and unnecessary tribunals. Occasionally, dismissal is the only option for staff who are particularly incompetent or whose behaviour is affecting their own and their colleague's performance as well, but in many situations you can actually help people in a kind way to see a way forward, to take responsibility, and the QLS technique is a great tool to use in this approach.

Chapter Seven

What makes a question good or bad?

First of all we can weed out some of the obvious bad ones. There are some common faults that most of us fall prey to when asking questions. Once we know them we can mentally put the delete pen through them.

One type to be wary of is the leading questions of the first type discussed in Chapter 5. We might also call them presumptuous or presupposing questions. These are questions that already carry the answer implicitly within them. In other words, you are all but telling the other person what you want them to answer. For example: "You don't like the way the department is organised, do you?" Or "Surely you must agree that this is the right thing to do?" These are effectively non-questions; they do not add to a communication and they tend to have a browbeating effect on the person being questioned. More to the point they do not ask the person questioned to think, enlarge upon a subject or do much more than nod in assent; so they have very limited use. Turning both of these examples into questions more likely to generate interesting answers you could ask: "What do you think of the way the department is organised?" and "What do you think we should do?"

Another one to avoid is what we might call the multiple choice question. This is where you ask a question that is in fact a number of questions and it becomes hard for the intended audience to know which question you want them to answer. For example; "Should we try Peter in another section, send him on a course or dismiss him?" The questioner is also doing too much of the work in this case and in similar ways to the presupposing question he is actually suggesting a series of answers and is limiting the audience's choice of answer by effectively restricting it to one of three options.

A faulty type of question that we may all find ourselves asking at some point is the embellished or embroidered question. This is a question that is usually occasioned by nervousness or over-eagerness to join in a discussion or conversation. Instead of asking one straightforward question we tend to string several together with the result that we can confuse the audience and will often find that we are greeted with a blank silence. For example: "Where are we going with this?...Do you think there is value in the action?...Is it a legitimate course to take?..." This is the kind of question we so often see in situations where people feel under pressure or short of time. The successful question is usually the one economical question that doesn't require a complex answer; the others are easily misunderstood, ignored or waved aside.

Also, be careful not to ask unanswerable questions. These are questions where the audience is asked about something that is completely outside their area of knowledge or experience. In interviews it can show an embarrassing lack of preparation on the part of the interviewer and in most situations it can only serve to make the other party feel uncomfortable because they are uncertain whether you wish them to make a comment or not. Worse still, they may not have the faintest idea what you are talking about.

Equally try to avoid using statements posing as questions. Examples are "Don't you think it would be good if we ... ?" and "Don't you think it is best to ... ?" These do not actually require a response and they do not add anything to a conversation or discussion. Mostly they tend to push forward the agenda of the questioner and ignore that of the person being questioned.

Sometimes without intending to we can find ourselves asking questions that have a detrimental effect – in particular they devalue the individual or audience we are addressing. Much will depend on the tone of voice we adopt but, if you do ask someone "Why did you do that?" be careful to ask it in the right tone, because it could sound judgemental. More obvious ones to steer clear of include "Why didn't you know that?" and "Can't you understand?"

Another detrimental type of question is one where you set out to be amusing and you hit the wrong note. At the early, banter stage of a conversation I have heard someone say "Hmmm. Dressed in black today – just been to a funeral?" and it turned out that was the case, and the deceased was a very close relative. And be careful with the use of jargon or technicalities in a question that your audience may not understand. Often by using complicated or in-house terms you are not only making assumptions about what the other person knows but you will appear arrogant.

Be careful too about the 'habit' questions. It is inevitable for people to have a few types of questions that they regularly deploy. It is a good idea to check these questions occasionally and use them appropriately. Habit questions will not necessarily serve you well and they may be appropriate for one situation but not for all. It is one of several reasons why sometimes having a third party present can be incredibly helpful.

For example on an interview panel – include someone who is not actually from the company. He or she will often ask an instinctive or even naïve question which will offer a new line of thought or a fresh perspective. The same approach applies to making a significant purchase or reaching a decision in your personal life. One habit question that I have heard time and time again at the close of an interview is "Is there anything you would like to ask us?" This is a poor question because it invariably comes at a point when the interviewer and the attendant panel are picking up their pens and notepaper or looking over towards the coffee machine. To most interviewees it appears as a question which is politely intended but which does not really want an answer. Consequently, you will often hear the response, "No thank you, that's fine." If you do want to hear the questions of the interviewee – and this can often be very enlightening – it is far more effective to make the question sound as if it means business and, use an open form, such as, "What would you like to ask us about the organisation or the appointment?"

Finally, in the list of obvious ones to avoid, look out for the question that starts open and ends closed. For example, "How do you feel about... Is it the right thing to do?" This is very common and it displays a tentativeness that can weaken your argument; it also lacks economy and directness, both of which are good qualities in questioning.

I am not proposing that all of these types of or approaches to questions should be universally avoided. Some of them do have their place in certain circumstances; much depends on the situation and the level of communication you have achieved with the audience. But, as a rule, these particular questions do not work well in negotiations, interviews, customer handling calls or meetings and situations where you are using questions to fact-find or otherwise conduct serious business. Also, if you think about some of the examples given here and examine the intention behind the question, you will usually be able to re-form them into far better questions that will generate better responses and make your audience feel much more comfortable.

But talking of 'far better questions' there are certain ingredients that will definitely help you to construct a good question.

What makes a good question?

There are a number of vital ingredients to a good question – or more particularly to *asking* a good question, because sometimes the question itself may be very direct and simple but as a result of your skill, it will be absolutely spot on and will transform the direction of a deal or a communication, or may become the catalyst for even greater change.

The ingredients of a good question:

- Timing
- Economy
- Intention
- Impact
- Inflection
- Intensity
- Relevance
- Legitimacy
- Surprise.

You will probably apply many of these qualities or attributes of a question quite naturally in the way you ask – but understanding them in a little more depth will make them part of your mental checklist and will strengthen your hand in any number of communications.

Timing

When you meet someone for the very first time you do not usually ask him or her "Where did you buy your suit?" or "What's wrong – you look a bit upset?" Such openers would rightly be considered impertinent and over-familiar. In the same way avoid easy or cheesy openers because your prospect, client or business associate may not be in the mood. As a rule, with a prospect or new customer or indeed in many situations with people with whom you may be on quite familiar terms, do not ask questions or try to engage in a way that is too familiar. This can be really off-putting. Over-familiarity tends to be the result of people making assumptions about various things, including the level of their friendship or acquaintanceship, what people find funny or interesting, and even what their politics or prejudices are. I want to re-emphasise that assumptions can kill communications stone dead. I've already mentioned the case of the top salesman who thought he'd clinched the deal by saying to my client, a brilliant entrepreneur "it's a win-win situation. It's a no-brainer." The result was the client's dismissal of the salesman.

Good timing is about asking questions that work appropriately at each stage of the journey that you take with your customer or other party gets properly underway. People tend to have their defences up at the beginning of a communication. This might apply if you are about to be interviewed or appraised, if you are sitting down to a negotiation, if you are about to be told the merits of a product or service by someone whose interest clearly lies in selling them to you, even if someone stops you in the corridor and says "May I ask you a question?" As the communication gets underway, you will relax, trust builds up and gradually a good questioner will introduce questions that match the level of communication you have achieved together.

In negotiations, the timing of questions is often the factor that will determine your success. You do not go in feet first with a question that you feel sure touches upon a weakness or sensitive area – you wait until you know the question will give you the most leverage. This is usually at a point when the other party may be feeling confident that they are on the homeward stretch and have a winning hand. So your timing in critical negotiations is a very important strategic element. In a completely different situation, when you are interviewing a candidate who appears excellent for the appointment but you have a question about what may be a sensitive health issue and how this may affect his or her ability to do the job, you must wait until you are confident that sufficient trust has been established between you before you pose this question.

Just as it is useful to carry a checklist of different types of question to ask, you will find that preparing an outline of the order of your key questions will help you to establish good timing. You should be flexible and intuitive too – but marshal your thoughts in advance.

Economy

It is good to aim for the shortest possible question that obtains the fullest possible answer. There is a great temptation when asking questions to provide too much context – to talk too much. Sometimes doing this betrays a lack of confidence on the part of the questioner, as if he or she is hesitant about asking a question. If you are a reporter looking for a serious answer to a serious question, it truly pays to keep the question short and unambiguous. The more you say, the more your respondent can turn your words to his advantage. If you are dealing with people who are highly experienced in answering questions, they will make mincemeat of a question that rambles across the countryside before coming to its point. Also the more you say the more your question is likely to be misinterpreted. "How can we make this work?" is far more powerful than, "There's no way we should be in this situation; the customer's screaming for a solution and if we don't give him one we'll all be for it, so what the heck are we going to do about it... and before you decide, let me tell you what I think..." and so on.

Economy of words is truly effective. What do you mean by that? How do you feel? Will this work? How will you achieve that? What issue are you referring to? Who is responsible for doing this? What can I do to improve the situation for you? These types of questions are direct and forceful because they are economical and likely to be respected.

Intention

The thing to ask yourself is "What do I want to achieve by asking this question?" This does not require a thorough or scientific analysis of each and every part of the conversation you are having but it is, once again, about being aware of the different types of question that you have at your disposal and how and when to use them to your advantage.

Each different type of question has a different intention behind it. Sometimes, for example, you will be looking for more details about a subject, so a probing question will help you to drill down into the subject matter. At another point, your intention may actually be to put your interviewee or customer at ease, so you will ask an easy, open type of question such as "What do you enjoy most in a typical working day?" or, in a different situation, "I'll do what I can – how can we help you?". Bear in mind that you can actually throw a conversation off course by asking a question that does not serve any purpose, or where the intention is unclear or might be misconstrued by the other party. In such a case, you may receive a negative or hostile reply.

I absolutely guarantee that having intentions that are honourable and not just short-sighted or self-serving will make all the difference.

Impact

Closely linked to intention is impact – which is to say, understanding the impact that the question will have on the person you are questioning. Again, this is about sensitivity to issues and remaining intuitive about the level of communication you are achieving as you unfold the subject and gather the information you seek. There is actually a set process in the way we connect with people through asking questions. First of all we engage and start to learn about the other person, or the particular situation; then we share our ideas; then we check our responses so that we are always careful to avoid making assumptions about what we are learning. Really effective questioning involves this process of questioning, listening, sharing and checking our responses.

Under the heading of impact we need to understand a little about human psychology to get the best results from our questions. In the process of our communications generally, we must try to learn what people's core concerns are, what really matters to them. If we can convey, through our questions, the sense that we value other people, that we appreciate them and are involving them in key processes, rather than railroading them, then our success in selling, persuading, communicating, negotiating, interviewing and so many other situations will improve dramatically.

Inflection

The way we ask a question, in terms of our phrasing and expression, has a huge effect on the response we receive. We should be thinking about inflection (rather than infliction) in the tone of our voice. As we relax, for example, during the process of an interview or discussion we may not be conscious of the fact that the interviewee is feeling that they have not done themselves justice in their responses so far and consequently is anything but relaxed. At such a stage, we might ask a question in a tone that we assume is easy and light and it can be taken entirely the wrong way. We may ask "What do you know about this project?" in such a way that it might be taken to mean that the interviewee clearly knows nothing about the subject. On the other hand, said in the right tone, this question is a perfectly straightforward enquiry.

A word of warning about the general tone of an interview: anything that steers an interview towards an interrogation is, in most circumstances, steering it the wrong way. In an interview situation, there are certain types of job that require particular skills and for these a highly rigorous and challenging approach may be most appropriate, but this is not the same as an interrogation. For example; candidates who are being interviewed for the work of answering phone calls from customers who may be extremely frustrated about a situation might excusably be subjected to an interview that tests their ability to handle highly emotional and potentially hostile customers. But if the purpose of the interview is to recruit the right people for this job, it is both typical and polite to explain something of the process beforehand.

Your intuition must also come into play. Interrogation is a perception; one individual may feel interrogated by a certain set of questions where another may not because so much depends on each person's confidence, well being, abilities and talents. But, in general, there is a distinct difference between a tough interview where you may work hard to find out a candidate's response to particular issues and an interrogation, which should remain the province of the police and other trained security personnel.

Intensity

I have, from time to time, used analogies of a journey and a ladder as applied, respectively, to a communication and the questioning process itself. Another factor in asking good questions is being able to graduate their intensity. The simple rule is to start with low intensity questions and move up gradually but the process does require practice, good listening and intuition. You have to feel your way as you take the journey and sometimes you will lower the pitch or intensity of the questions in order to slow the pace while, at other times, if you feel you are trusted and have caught the imagination of your audience, you can climb higher and probe further. It is useful to remember that, even if you are working with a prepared script – such as in a sales situation – you must listen carefully to the responses you are getting and be prepared to change your tack.

Relevance

If you want to guide the course of a communication towards a particular end your questions need to be increasingly relevant as the journey continues. The relevance of your question demon-strates your insight and it also shows that you are listening to the other party and taking real note of what they are saying, what they want to achieve and how you can help them. So, the more relevant you make your questions, the more a customer will feel valued and the more they will trust your judgement. Conversely, if you are in a situation where you are trying to appease a customer who is very frustrated by a failure in a service or a product or if you are in negotiations and at a critical moment an irrelevant remark or question is like throwing petrol on a fire.

Surprise

What else is in the goody bag? Ah yes – the element of surprise. Surprising someone with a question is a great way of making headway in most communications. A surprising question takes various forms. It can be a very astute question that goes right to the heart of a complex matter and therefore immediately enlivens the interest of the person being questioned. Usually, you will know you have surprised the other person because he or she will often respond with "That's a good question". In another situation you may be testing the imagination and quick-wittedness of an interviewee by throwing out a line that is obviously intended humorously, "What would you do with a million ping pong balls?" In most areas of business communications, surprise questions can be used to make people look at a problem or issue from a completely different perspective. Sometimes just asking "What would you do if you were in my shoes?" is enough to give a spur to the communication.

If you have a good surprise question up your sleeve, or one pops into mind, remember to make a note of it – so often the right moment will pass or you will forget the question itself. As with all good questions the surprise one demands your attention to timing, intensity, inflection, impact, economy, relevance – all the ingredients that are in your power to shape your question and truly hit the mark.

Chapter Eight

How can we answer questions more effectively?

You will find that the more you practise and improve your questioning skills, the more you are likely to improve your ability to answer questions skilfully too. Part of the reason for this is that there are similarities in the techniques involved in both types of communication.

When people are asked a question, perhaps even if they are anticipating being asked a challenging or awkward question, they often show three types of response: they avoid the question or try to skirt round it; they freeze; or they decide to give an instant response. All three approaches are less than helpful if you are seeking to provide a really impressive answer. As part of your list of checks and balances, it is well worth remembering that you can significantly improve your ability to respond effectively to questions by applying the following simple techniques.

First of all, don't answer. That is to say do not respond instantly. Most people rush into an answer and even if you are very confident that you have the answer ready and can just push the verbal button, you will benefit by establishing a pause. A three-second pause will help you to marshal your thoughts and to make your pitch clearly and firmly. In an interview situation, in an appraisal, in a negotiation – in any situation where the question may have some weight and importance – the three-second delay, (or even longer if you feel comfortable) is perfectly acceptable; it is an overt demonstration that you are giving the question proper consideration. As a result, the pause will usually add to the overall impression that you should want to make, which is that you think carefully and are keen to exercise good judgement. This is a bonus in your favour in an interview or conversation with the boss and it is also likely to make a sensitive interviewer respond with more considered and well spaced questions. So, as in the QLS technique, here we see the immense value and potency of silence.

Another tool for responding to questions is one that is broadly adopted by politicians, particularly those who are frequently questioned by the media. The technique they often adopt is not to answer directly but to use some of the ingredients of the question to explain the key points of their own agenda – to say what they want to say. Sometimes politicians can infuriate listeners and viewers by blatantly ignoring a question and then starting to unpack their stall instead. There is a happy medium between this approach and the one I'm suggesting which is to answer the question and include the content that supports the communication objectives that you need to achieve.

To do this effectively, in an interview or negotiation for example, you need to be well prepared with questions, answers, facts and evidence that directly serve your purpose. Bear in mind that, in interviews particularly, it is not just you who wants the interview to go well – the interviewer does too and they have a substantial amount of work to do. The more you can prepare for an interview by considering a wide range of topics of the kind that you may be asked and by noting and rehearsing your answers, the more you will support the interviewers' role and doing this will help to differentiate you from competing candidates. You will also give yourself the best possible chance to shine.

The best interpersonal communications are a dialogue, not a one-way pitching of ideas. I cannot overemphasise the benefit that candidates will achieve by preparing really thoroughly – being hard on yourself if necessary, to make sure you cover all the ground in advance – and by using your own influence to steer the course of the discussion. Most candidates are not even aware that in an interview they too, can ask questions, unless they are invited. This is not the case. Naturally, it is respectful to choose your moments and to ask permission to ask a question but, in general, the more you can find out about the role that you may be taking in an organisation the better placed you are to present your skills, talents and experience accordingly. It is a question of believing in yourself.

What kind of questions might you usefully ask at most interviews? Well, the following are a few that, as an interviewer, I would be impressed to hear and pleased to try and answer:

- Can I ask some questions to make sure that I understand the role is and what you are looking for?
- Why are you recruiting now?
- What skills do you really need to succeed in this role?
- What do I need to demonstrate so that you hire me?
- What difficulties have you had with other people in this role?
- When do you need to have someone in position, and why is this date important?

One way to help in this preparation is to imagine you are the interviewer and then draw up a set of questions that you think you would ask yourself. By doing this a few times before the interview you will be very likely to cover themes and subjects that will come up on the day. When such questions do come up, do not leap in with your answer immediately, as if to say "I know this one", but apply the three seconds of silence rule to show you are considering the matter wisely before giving your account.

Do not just ask a few questions. Do not be shy to respond by asking a clarifying question if there is the slightest doubt about the focus of the subject in question. Sometimes a clarifying question can be impressive because it might demonstrate that you know about the subject in some depth and need to refine the focus to be able to discuss a particular area. Also, by asking a clarifying question you will buy yourself further time to assemble your thoughts. Be interested in the responses and probe further. In this way you and the interviewer are both helped substantially.

Another useful tool, particularly in response to a challenging question, is to compliment the questioner. Mostly people do this instinctively by saying "That's a good question" or "I think you've hit the nub of the issue" – but whether instinctive or not, this type of response, used sparingly, shows graciousness and is pleasing to the questioner. Again, this response buys you a little extra precious time.

The common theme in these approaches to responding is finding your own pace and taking your time to prepare an answer that does you justice. At the heart of this process is the considered silence. I vividly recall how this worked for me in one quite challenging situation. I was in a training session when a salesperson asked me point blank what I would do if I was being thrown out of a building by the owner who tells you he does not want you back. The process I followed was to be silent – I did not answer the question but let it sink in. As a result others in the room chipped in and I soon learned more background to the situation. Apparently, the salesperson was new to the company and the previous salesperson had been fired for letting down customers on all sorts of fronts, including rudeness. By remaining silent and gathering that information I was able to come up with a considered answer. I said that in that situation you should ask politely for the business owner's advice and say, "I need your help. What has my company done to make you feel like this?"

This takes us right back to the key questioning skills of fact finding and showing interest. By doing this, the salesperson is not trying to get back in through the door; instead he is genuinely showing interest in the customer and he creates an opportunity to learn something important, make the customer feel valued and create the opportunity to turn the situation around. In response to such an aggressive approach from a business owner many people might be tempted to put on their coats and walk away but this is a negative response and rather like slamming the door on an argument, it achieves nothing and leaves both sides in a negative emotional state.

Over many years I have noticed some questions which constantly recur. They do so because they are usually rewarding to ask in an interview and they are perhaps the questions that we should all take time to think about. The questions themselves are straight-forward but I have seen them provoke quite stressed responses in interviewees, in particular the desire to make an instant answer, which is often unclear as a result. As interviewees realise they are hashing up their responses they also tend to add and qualify and fuss their thinking, digging themselves into even deeper holes. I thought it might be useful to turn the tables on myself and provide some answers to some of the more challenging questions that are asked many times and are too often answered poorly.

How do you handle a difficult manager?

It is quite common for employees to find themselves under pressure because of a manager's behaviour toward them. The first thing they must do is recognise that this is happening; it will cause stress and too much stress clouds the mind, impairs judgement and has a bad effect on performance. But we need to remember that managers are human beings too, and ultimately what sits between the manager and you is the relationship. It is your responsibility as much as your manager's to make an investment to build this relationship, if there are issues and problems occurring.

To illustrate this I ask people on training courses how many of the audience would like more encouragement and better feedback from their managers – usually most hands go up. I then ask how many give encouragement or praise to their manager or provide feedback to him or her. Very few hands tend to go up. So rule number one is to understand the meaning of two-way traffic.

In dealing with a difficult manager we need to know what he or she expects, what is not working, and we need to challenge our own attitude to make sure that it is a 'can do' not a 'can't do' one. We also need to make a proper effort to invest in the relationship in order to achieve clarity of communication and find out what has gone off track. If we allow ourselves to sink into a victim mentality then we will be disempowered and this will cause a downward cycle of stress and poor performance.

The golden rule is to look at the problem from a positive perspective, not to focus on what is bad but to find the good or better aspects of the situation. If you persist in thinking that your manager is incompetent, that his requests are unreasonable, or dwelling on other such thoughts, the negativity will make the situation much worse. Remember that the bigger the challenge, the bigger the opportunity to achieve a positive outcome. It might help if you imagine you are going to leave the organisation because of your situation and then imagine you are being interviewed for another position and being asked why you left your last job. When you answer that you left because you had a difficult relationship with your manager, you are then asked what you did to improve the situation. If you can't answer that question satisfactorily in such a scenario it is not going to greatly impress your potential new employer – or yourself.

So the short answer is to realise what is going on. Be positive about it and discard the negative thoughts. Avoid playing the victim and realise that it is equally your responsibility, no matter where you are in the organisation, to invest in the relationship, to help to repair and build it. Do not see feedback and encouragement as a one-way process. If you go into a new role with these positive approaches it is unlikely that your manager will find fault with you in a way that will have any lasting or problematic effect. It also helps, incidentally, if you do not view your career as a nine-to-five job but as a key part of your life that affects your health, wealth and well being. When you look at it this way you will soon realise the importance of investing in good relationships.

If your manager is simply impossible to work with, then it's essential that you take your problem to the highest level and ask for help. Here again questions will help you. If you are demanding and unprepared, you are unlikely to be successful. No employer wants to lose a high performing employee.

Sometimes the best thing to do is to find alternative employment. But don't burn your bridges, you may need a reference in the future or even want to return if the grass isn't as green over there as it appeared.

I can remember one business owner who at our very first meeting showed me a letter of complaint from an employee. "Read this and tell me what you think". So I did, twice in fact. The lady concerned had written a very well constructed letter about what he was doing that made her feel uncomfortable. After some consideration and some fact finding questions to set the scene for the letter I told him how impressed I was that she felt able to approach him in this way and that she was offering very constructive suggestions. The response I received made it very clear why his employee was unhappy. It was easy for me to walk away considering how much that business was losing through the owner's insecurity and his failure to listen to and involve his people.

How do you deal with difficult colleagues?

Essentially this is about negotiation, the first stage of which is consulting and listening. This means asking questions to understand the other party's perspectives and to learn what's needed or lacking, in order to ease a situation and improve the relationship. Conversely, if we become defensive because of a colleague's behaviour or attitude, or if we go into battle, we will aggravate matters.

Looking at the psychological factors behind such a situation, the difficulties that people experience are often the result of stress. Are they not attaining what they want to, are they are they worried about what they are achieving or perhaps afraid of the consequences of failure?

The best way to help people calm down, or turn themselves round, is to demonstrate appreciation by asking questions calmly, to help them give vent to the real issues and problems that may be troubling them. This is not a passive approach but a highly proactive and effective use of your skills. The other good thing about this approach is that it can reveal unseen opportunities to achieve better results. It is possible that your question will spark acknowledgement in your colleague; for example, he or she will suddenly realise what your agenda is supportive rather than threatening. Demonstrating appreciation is the vital part in this process; it introduces calmness and it allows time for people to digest and understand issues that may be troubling.

Most important of all, realise that you have incredible power to influence others if you choose to use it. The QLS technique is very powerful when dealing with difficult colleagues, particularly when they make you feel stressed or even angry. Use questions, listening and a good amount of silence, this will help you and your colleague to reflect and agree the way forward.

Over the years I have seen many teams with a 'sub-culture' that is bitter and unhelpful and normally created by one or two people. It's important that you are seen as someone with a positive out-look, someone who looks at the bigger picture and doesn't get bogged down in the small things, the details. Try to avoid the petty, rankling feelings that focus on blame or the other person's shortcomings. Move on, go the extra mile, be generous. I so often encounter this 'pettiness' in teams where a team leader is in a position that's beyond their ability or frustrated by his team or visa versa and instead of looking at all the truly positive goals, activities, skills and talents that they all share, they dwell on unappealing details. By adopting a more mature forward thinking attitude, you will be leading by example. This is a time for you to be politically astute to ensure that you are seen by your employer as an asset rather than a liability to the team.

How do you resolve conflicts in a team?

Conflict resolution in a team requires good leadership. First of all you must recognise what is happening – you'd be surprised how often people do not. Then be determined to do something about it, because a conflict situation only rarely peters out if you choose to ignore it.

The next thing is to understand exactly what is going on and talk to all those involved to learn where the problem resides. Use the QLS technique to draw people out at this stage, asking questions calmly and without judgement. Be sure to listen very carefully. If you ascertain that the problem involves just two particular members of the team, talk to them separately applying the same questioning, listening and silence technique. As a leader it is also essential that you make the consequences of not achieving a resolution to this conflict crystal clear to everyone in the team. Let them know how and why the conflict will debilitate the productivity, performance and general well being of the team.

Your calmness and maturity will be very influential but you must make sure that you understand the problem and that the people involved have been properly and fully heard. There is a wonderful example of the importance of this in Native American Indian culture where tribal elders get together and the person talking holds a 'talking stick'. He does not pass this on to anyone else until he feels sure that his view has been properly heard by the others. Meanwhile, the others are bound to hold their silence and be attentive.

Without the aid of a talking stick, you must be a good facilitator and use your questioning and listening skills to draw people out. Make sure you create the right environment for the important discussions, somewhere quiet and sympathetic. You might offer tea, coffee and biscuits. In some situations it will pay to involve two conflicting team members in a discussion at the end of a working day and then take them both out for dinner – and watch the problem evaporate.

How do you deal with unfair criticism?

Again, first understand the effect the unfair criticism is having on you. If it hurts badly and makes you feel like reacting defensively be aware that these emotions will not help. Also, give close thought to the criticism to see if there is any value in it because it may well be constructive criticism that is put across in a way that unintentionally hurts you. If, however, you know that the motive is malign and that a game is being played by the person doing the criticising, or they are venting their own negative feelings on you, then avoid playing the game at all costs.

Most constructive is to adopt the QLS technique and use questions to try to disarm the person. Another factor is timing. Do not necessarily try to deal with the criticism straightaway, on the same day. But when you first receive the criticism see if you can muster the dignity and calmness to reply along the lines of "Thank you very much, I will take that on board and think about it."

Bear in mind that criticism, however intended, can be a catalyst for change and improvement. Over the years I've received criticism for which I remain very grateful. There have even been times when I've had very hostile remarks made which I felt were unfair. On one occasion I provided a delegate I was training with some constructive criticism and received a very aggressive response. As a direct result of this I redesigned a particular training model with a highly positive effect. Later I met the woman again and she was very apologetic about what she'd said and told me she had taken my comments on board. So we had both gained from the situation.

In general, when I realise I am about to receive criticism I have a sense of instinctive fear somewhere in the gut, but I always tell myself that this is going to be good for me. This always calms me down and reduces the likelihood of a defensive reaction. We've all got to have pride in ourselves and a sense of purpose in what we do, but we must also have humility.

Sometimes it will help if you bring another person, a trusted colleague, a supervisor or co-director, into the frame. They will help you to decide about the nature of the criticism and your response to it. They may even reinforce the criticism, in which case it is likely that it is meant constructively and you need to take notice. An impartial view from a third party is invaluable at times when emotions are running high.

What are your weaknesses?

This is a question I've asked on numerous occasions and while it may not be the best question in the toolkit it invariably produces interesting answers – and ones that throw light on the character of a candidate. It never ceases to amaze me how many people have no weaknesses whatsoever while others will answer the question with coy suggestions that they have been told they work too hard or that they're too committed to their job.

Inevitably, the degree of frankness that you decide upon in answering this question is up to you. My view is that the truth is the sharpest tool in the box and my experience is that it often pays to tell the truth and to be as candid as you can. Honesty and a degree of humility are both qualities that employers tend to look for in most candidates; they demonstrate that you have a good degree of self-awareness, that you want to learn and that you are considerate about others. Your candidness will also build a degree of trust in an interview situation.

One proviso is that when you report on your weaknesses, you do not admit to every possible shortcoming in the book – this is likely to be unbelievable and is too self-deprecating by half. Try and be specific and choose a weakness that you can verify, perhaps one that your friends or former supervisors have pointed out to you. Also important, when you disclose a weakness you should provide some information on what you are actively doing to combat its effect and improve upon the situation.

For example, you may, like me, be very impatient, always wanting to get things done immediately and possibly not ticking all the boxes needed to meet the goal most successfully. Your reply might include the fact that you are very aware of this failing and that you have empowered your team to report to you if they believe you are being impatient and that you are also doubly conscious of ensuring the checks and balances are used to ensure you have not rushed the gates. As another example, you might be a highly creative individual but someone who lacks organisational thoroughness. If this is the case, you need to make sure you explain what you are doing about this shortcoming, how you are trying to improve, perhaps by introducing disciplines into your working day that will harness your creativity and enhance your organising abilities.

When you answer this question try to be concise. Interviewers do not want the story of your life or a dramatic account of how and why you came to be the person you are. In general, bear in mind that your honesty will be appreciated and any attempt to make yourself look like one of the many 'perfect' people I've met at interviews in the past will be spotted for what they are – either evasive or lacking in self-awareness.

How do you deal with difficult customers?

When someone is in an unhappy or negative state of mind it is not possible to negotiate with them with any degree of success – so the first thing to do is to recognise there is a problem. You will help to calm a customer down if you are calm yourself, and listen carefully to what they have to say and then ask questions to make sure you have heard the full story. If you rush in too quickly and point out that they are wrong or find discrepancies in their account of a situation, you will only pour fuel on the fire. The classic technique to apply at this stage is to listen. Another approach is to replay what the customer has said to you and then ask if you have understood the story correctly. Then ask if there is anything else you should know. This fact-finding approach demonstrates that you are concerned about the issue and that you value the customer.

In a protracted situation, make sure you and the customer can take a break – do not try to go for a quick fix. Be very aware that just providing a scripted answer such as "These are our rules, there is nothing more we can do for you" will result in a broken relationship and a very unhappy customer. Another powerful approach is to create options. Sit down with the customer and discuss what the options are to solving the situation and then offer the customer a choice. Finally, get a commitment from the customer to the agreed way forward and also make sure that the solution you are offering is one that can be achieved. At this point you can give commitments.

If you want to go the extra mile remember to thank the customer for bringing the situation to your attention and tell them what you have learned – and do this in a way that does not sound as if it is from a script. The more genuine and spontaneous you are the more the customer will respond positively.

Always make sure that customers are kept informed and know exactly what is going to happen and when. Don't focus on what you can't do, don't blame anyone or anything but find out what you can do. Asking yourself, the customer and your colleagues questions will help you to do this. And always deliver on your promises.

What do you do when people will not listen to you?

The reason people do not listen is because they don't want to – and this is because there is something else on their mind . So there is a block and the best way to remove that block is to ask questions and demonstrate your own interest and appreciation by listening intently to what they have to say. At all costs do not try to impose your views on them or try to make them listen.

An example of this in my experience was a time when I was consulting and a business leader had very strong views about what he wanted to do in order to solve a particular situation. His general approach suggested that he was very unlikely to have any interest in anything I might think. I knew that if I tried to share what I thought with him before he had fully unloaded his own mind on the subject I would have no possibility of making any headway. So I listened intently, remained silent and then asked questions, gradually introducing an alternative perspective.

By listening and understanding we can remove the block and start to share and we will then build a better relationship and a better outcome. Again, it is about taking the initiative and responsibility, not being a victim and equally not forcing your view on others. You do this by taking control of the process that will ultimately lead to effectively influencing the person who isn't listening to you.

Chapter Nine

Where do we go from here?

I feel sure that a picture has emerged in which the question mark occupies a dominant position. I hope by now that we can agree that making use of questions more frequently can have a hugely beneficial influence on our work and lives, on other people and on all manner of situations. All we need to do individually is to practise and to apply questions and questioning techniques every day on ourselves and with others. As part of this we must learn how to improve our listening, keep our silence, and give consideration to the way we respond to the questions of others.

Whoever you are and whatever you do, I believe you have a responsibility to contribute, to influence and to share by asking questions. If you have a supervisory position – whatever your level of seniority – you are in a position to ensure that questions, listening, learning and giving feedback become part of the culture. Then just watch the improvements in performance, productivity and profits.

I passionately believe that if you consistently use questions and apply some simple questioning techniques you will improve both your happiness and your personal relationships – two areas of our lives that tend to be the focus of most of our activity and energy.

With that focus in mind I want to look at a few questions that I think will help us all to transform our attitudes and empower us to improve our lives. It doesn't matter what you may have already achieved in life, I firmly believe that personal development is a continuous process. The right questions will help you to make major changes and ensure the right direction of travel.

I am also going to look at the position of feedback in our lives and will underline just how important it is that we engage in feedback, take it seriously and are prepared for it.

I would strongly advise that you make notes and checklists, underline heavily and scribble in the margins of this book. Then perhaps later make yourself some checklists about learning points. I do this generally and just by noting something down I remember it better and I find myself applying the idea usefully in different situations.

First, having done the rounds of many types of question, I would like to stop for a moment and consider one certainly open question that I believe is the most powerful of all of them.

What – is the ultimate question

You will have noticed that throughout this book I have flagged up open questions in preference to closed questions. Generally, I do believe in the immense value of open questions but I would stress that closed questions can also be used with very positive effect in all kinds of communication. They are great for extracting details; they are very useful for closing interviews and also for punctuating different stages of communications.

This said, if I were to choose the question that I think has the most value and usefulness I would choose an open question that begins with the word 'what'. In my experience the 'what' question evokes a much broader response from the recipient than any other open question. 'What' is used more often than not in questions that work as catalysts, helping people to think creatively. What can we do? What's possible? What is the best approach to take? We can be philosophical with the 'what' question or we can use it to ask the kind of question to which in our business or personal lives, we will keep returning and which will keep generating new answers and values. My recommendation is to hold the 'what' question as a tool to be deployed strategically.

On many occasions I have observed people struggling to come up with a good question when they are in the thick of a difficult situation or negotiation – when the pressure is really on. In my training I often demonstrate a simple but effective tool that will help you through such a blockage. Say "what" out loud to yourself quickly; imagine that the word has a piece of string attached to your sub-conscious mind and that when you say the word it pulls the string and engages thoughts and ideas. You quite literally start with no idea but soon you have formed a question. It may not be the best question in the world but, by practising this technique on your own, you will find that, in time, you will come up with a whole sequence of 'what' questions. What else do you need to know? What can I tell you about...? What do you most value about...? What do you want to achieve most from this discussion? Practise this and you will be surprised how effective it can be. When you do this, another useful tip is to flick as spontaneously and easily as you like from subject to subject, simply asking 'what'.

Another really critical point about being stuck in a communication and not knowing what to ask next is not to try too hard to come up with a great question. You will be surprised how many poor questions can trigger great responses or those that stimulate you very quickly to find a far better question to ask next.

So the ultimate question begins with "what" – and what we are going to look at in the rest of this chapter is the way in which you can use the 'what' question with a series of other open and closed questions to help in your life, career and relationships.

Health, wealth and happiness

Just as a business can provide an anchor for its long term strategy by developing a vision, so each of us will benefit enormously by setting ourselves goals. And we start the process quite simply by asking ourselves what we consider to be important in our lives.

This is a question that becomes increasingly poignant and perhaps important to ask as time goes by, because time is probably the most precious commodity we have and the older you are the more astonished you are by the rapidity of its passing. No matter the time frame that we set when we give ourselves specific goals, the essential thing is that we are imposing an outline structure to work with. For example, I may set myself the goal to grow my business profitability by 30 per cent within two years, or within four years; either way, I set myself a target and I make myself accountable for achieving it.

I choose the heading 'health, wealth and happiness' because this can encapsulate many types of goal. What makes us healthy? Our food intake, the quality of what we eat, the amount of oxygen we take into our lungs, the level and extent of exercise that we do regularly – these all important but what is most influential on our health is our mental well being. The decisions we make and the actions we take have a direct bearing on this. My argument is that we can shape and inform our mental well being to beneficial effect by the questions we ask ourselves, not just at the cross-roads and pressured times of our lives, but regularly and as a matter of daily practice.

And what makes us wealthy? Wealth will mean different things to different people – to many it is about money, to others it is a measure of sporting success, the happiness of the family, the achievement of other goals. For the purposes of focus let's look at wealth from a financial perspective, because ultimately money is important – at least the lack of it is sufficiently upsetting to mean that we should all take money seriously and treat it with respect.

People have a varied attitude towards money. Some people like it and can't get enough of it; some people do not know how to use it to their advantage and have little interest in how to do this; others avoid the subject at all costs because it is too painful to deal with.

Perhaps if we are preparing ourselves for some serious goal-setting we should ask ourselves what our attitude to money is and why it is that way. If we are people who see the pursuit of money as the ultimate goal in life and the real meaning of success then we might ask ourselves several questions. What is our money for? Are we spending it wisely? Are there other things in our lives that we are overlooking in our eagerness to pursue this objective? Are there people we are overlooking in this particular chase?

If we are among those who do not have an interest or do not know how to use money to our advantage, we probably need to take a little stock of where this approach might lead us. Does our lack of interest in money affect our lives now or will it in the future? Have we made sufficient provisions for the future? Are there ways of balancing our general lack of interest with ways of achieving financial security in the longer term?

And for those of us who would prefer not even to think of money because it is generally too painful to do so, there are other questions we should ask. In fact, these are the types of questions that all of us may at some time want to ask ourselves because the feeling of being overwhelmed by financial problems is much the same as the feeling of being overwhelmed by all types of emotional or physical upheavals.

In such a situation we need to focus on what is positive about the situation not what is negative. I have used this approach in countless situations with clients who are experiencing difficulties. I have even helped someone whose husband was suffering from cancer and received some very humbling advice from the woman who shared with me what was good about the things she was going to do to make her husband's life more comfortable. (Why is it that often the most terrible circumstances can bring out the best in people?)

But in terms of financial pain it is extremely common for people to do their utmost to avoid their financial responsibilities when things start to go wrong. Perhaps they have too much debt, loans need to be repaid, and credit cards are at their borrowing limits. The way to change this is actually to deepen your frustration by recognising the consequence of not paying your debts. Ask yourself, what are the consequences? What will happen to me and my family if I don't? Write these consequences down. Then write down the consequences of paying the debts back. How will you feel about achieving full repayment? What do you need to do achieve this? What will you gain by it? Then make a commitment to yourself and take action; and, if you are the type who will let yourself off the hook, make a commitment which involves someone else. The other person does not need to be your closest friend or loved one; they can be someone else with whom you can share the problem and to whom you will make yourself accountable. In my experience confiding in another person can be the deal-maker.

Sometimes it is not just a question of financial pressure but other fundamental things that come between us and a happy life, such as stress and lack of confidence. There are questions that will help you deal with these, too, that we will come on to here. But let's put the picture of our lives into a little more in context.

I want you to imagine that there are three types of people: those who drift along letting life happen to them, a kind of 'what will be will be' attitude; those who live in fear and worry about what's going to happen next; and those who strive to change things and achieve things to make a difference. Perhaps it is fair to say that most people want to be in the third category. In my opinion many people can be counted in this category – at least for significant parts of their lives – because so many of us simply do not realise what contribution we make. We are all connected to each other in a highly complex web of social and working activity and our decisions and actions do make a difference – if only we could be aware of our own contributions, talent and skills. In my customer service training this is a key teaching point: that everyone in the organisation really matters, whatever their level. From one point of view you could argue that people at the frontline are more important than the CEO of the company – my apologies to all CEOs but I think they would understand the gist of the argument.

I think the reality is that many of us tend to drift through life. Things happen to us and we almost sleepwalk through the daily and weekly cycle of repeated events. The Monday morning blues come round again and the in-tray piles high, or the job interview is looming on the horizon and we have been out of work for three months – and how do I know that this is not just going to be another waste of my time? All of us, in different stages and situations, need to kick-start our lives to get into a really positive frame of mind so that we can move forward and get back in control. This is where I would like to share with you some really positive questions that have helped in my life.

A few years ago I experienced I highly traumatic breakdown in a business relationship. As it happened I was in a position to take revenge on a particular individual in such a way that could have caused him immense damage. I had the choice of either doing this or moving on and putting the trouble behind me. I chose the latter route although I was severely tempted to get my own back. To make the decision I asked myself, "What do I want to do? What's good about taking revenge? What will I gain by it ? What will I gain on the other hand by leaving the situation be? How will I feel about myself if I do not take revenge?"

Closing the door on the situation and leaving it behind me not only proved to be the right decision but, as a result, opened up untold and amazing new opportunities for me. Quite literally, a new chapter started in my life; I was in a much brighter place and this all owed to the initial question, "What do I want to do?"

We have used this question in negotiations where there has been deep conflict and relationship breakdown, where things have gone out of control and small issues have been blown out or proportion. By asking the question "What is the right thing to do now?" we have helped people to think more clearly and to work together to find a way forward.

In essence, what makes us healthier is our thinking. This effects how we feel and our feelings effect how we perform and what we achieve. The way to change our thinking and our feelings is to ask ourselves supportive, encouraging, empowering questions.

Too often we will bring the wrong kind of question to the table – questions like "What's going to go wrong if I do this/don't do this? I recall one very successful entrepreneur talking on the radio and making the very apt point that the trouble with having so much experience is that he can see everything that might go wrong in a situation – and that can inhibit entrepreneurial decision-making.

Focusing on what might go wrong will debilitate us. "What can go wrong if I put my hand up at work and say, this needs to change?" "What could wrong if I go home and have a conversation with my spouse and ask what do we need to do differently to have a healthier relationship?"

We must not focus too much on what can wrong but on what can go right. We need to focus on what is good for us and for the people around us. If we maintain the principle of thinking along the lines of what is good for everyone this will help us and those in our orbit to work together and create a brighter future. It will also continuously empower us to face whatever challenges fall in our path.

So the inner game, the mental process, really matters if we seek to make changes, to achieve or to move forwards from a situation of stalemate. We need to keep four fundamental questions about our feelings inscribed in our minds and hearts:

- How am I feeling?
- Why am I feeling this way?
- How do I want to feel?
- How will that help me?

This will help us to meet challenges and confront problems. So, for example; How am I feeling? Annoyed. Why? Because this person is doing this, this and this. How do I want to feel? Calm and relaxed. How will that help me? I'll be able to influence them better, to think better, control the situation and stop this person from making me feel bad. Or I'll be able to move ahead with my career, I'll be able to get that job, I'll make that sale, I'll negotiate that deal, achieve a pay rise, enjoy a profit share. It's all to do.

So the inner game is critically important. It helps us to steel ourselves; it will strengthen our resolve and open our minds. What is also incredibly important is to have some reasonable understanding of how we come across to other people and how we might improve this. Many of us are acutely self-aware, while others are utterly oblivious of the way they present themselves. It pays handsomely to involve other people and to ask for feedback to achieve a full understanding of what we are really like and how we present ourselves to other people. I seek feedback regularly in my training but you can do it individually by involving a trusted partner or friend who can help you to realise what your strengths and weaknesses really are.

By seeking and preparing ourselves for feedback we will learn the answer to the deeply rooted question 'What holds us back?' It is essential to find someone who will give us honest feedback and to be prepared for it – bear in mind that our success in life and work is dependent upon relationships. They require us to show:

- Generosity
- Appreciation
- Understanding
- Honesty
- Intimacy
- Forgiveness
- Accountability

And because the feedback we gain is potentially so valuable to our success we must be willing to do a number of things:

- Make people feel safe so that they give us completely honest feedback and advice
- Acknowledge the other person's perspective and experience
- Receive the feedback, be vulnerable and take risks
- Say thank you for it, without debating, defending or justifying
- Acknowledge faults

- Consider the feedback we don't want
- Tell the other person what we plan to do with the feedback

It is quite normal to resist change but instead we should ask questions and listen. Not everyone will have the right experience and knowledge to provide this kind of feedback, so we must find people we respect; perhaps those who can advise on specific issues.

To achieve really useful feedback, some of the questions you might ask include:

1 What do I do that's stopping me from making progress?
2 What are the things that I need to do so that I can achieve my full potential?
3 What do I do that you dislike?
4 What do I do that you value?
5 Why is that?

We must allow people to reflect on these questions and not interrupt their responses. By asking open, clarifying questions and by demonstrating our appreciation we will truly value the experience. If we avoid developing these kinds of relationship and asking for this level of feedback we can limit our performance and success.

This type of feedback can help us to develop a wonderful quality - self-awareness and an awareness of the impact that we have on people and situations. Critical feedback might help you to focus on some areas of your character where you might want to do some work, or at least monitor yourself. For example:

- Self-doubt
- Inflexible thinking
- Pessimism
- Perfectionism

- Risk avoidance
- Conflict avoidance
- Difficulty in trusting others
- Micro-managing
- Trying too hard
- Laziness
- Not listening
- Defensiveness
- Not communicating
- Not committing
- Expecting too much
- Being impatient

I firmly believe that most people fail to achieve a fraction of their potential. Many of us bury our potential as a result of our own lack of confidence, or allow it to be buried by others. Some people set out in life with hopes of achieving something special only to be told by people in their own families, close friends or loved ones that they should not follow that route because they may be disappointed. These 'supportive' people think they are being helpful but their desire to protect their loved ones results in smothering them, and they will hold them back. This kind of feedback is not what anyone needs. If you have a particular desire or ambition it is often the ember that displays a hidden talent and can be the spark to ignite a growing skill and propel you on a journey of success. The challenge for all of us is to recognise the hard facts of reality and understand what we are good at and what we are not good at. It is also important that we face up to the problem of being held back by people who, for many different reasons, are actively trying to disempower us. This can be a partner, spouse, colleague or friend.

If you know you are being held back or inhibited, you have the choice of either putting your head down and letting people exercise their will and control or of moving forward and following your own path. Ask the questions; What is the right thing to do for me...for them...for the future? What do I gain by following my own path? What can I do to make them understand that this is important to me? How will I feel if I confront this situation?

Not making the necessary changes to overcome obstacles such as these is often down to our lack of self-confidence. This issue comes up frequently in my dealings with trainees and others. Many years ago I had a distinct problem with self-confidence as a result of working with someone who was really disempowering me. He was brilliant at what he did but I always found that he would adopt the high ground in every interaction we had and my perspective was not listened to. One day I asked myself, what can I do to really build up my confidence? I took a block of post-it notes and wrote down on each page something that I had achieved or something I was good at. The trick here is to let the mind free, rather like brainstorming, and not to make judgements about what comes out – so the ideas flow. For me, the result was a huge mixture of comments including trivial and important things.

I absolutely guarantee that you can fill up a block of post-it notes, page by page, in this way. When I had finished I stuck all the notes on a wall and there in front of me, on both close and ad hoc inspection I had a very upbeat version of me. I looked at this and considered that here was actually a very capable person, someone who has a lot to offer. It really helped. Once again, it will help you to add to these notes about yourself by involving someone else, to prompt you and add their own perspective.

While lack of confidence can inhibit us substantially, stress is a particular problem for many people and can lead not only to poor work performance but ultimately to ill health. At work it is very often caused by trying to do things that you know you cannot do. If you find yourself in this situation, ask for help. Do not be afraid to do this. Asking for help might go against the grain because you think it betrays incompetence or lack of confidence but it actually demonstrates the opposite. If you are in an organisation where you know you cannot operate without that help, and it is not forthcoming, then it is probably time to look for a position elsewhere. But before you take that step, ask the questions a number of times to see if you can influence the organisation and help them see the value of supporting you. Most organisations, large and small, genuinely do want to help.

We can use questions to tackle our own stress in several ways. One of the first and most important objectives is to recognise that we are stressed in a debilitating way. We live in stressful times and we may be mistaken for believing that everyone is in exactly the same space as we are, when the truth is we may be suffering an unacceptably high level of stress. It never ceases to amaze me how many people struggle to recognise their own feelings. But living in denial of stress carries with it the prospect of exhausting our bodies and shattering our mental well being. In stressful circumstances the sub-conscious mind seems to battle on 24/7 and we cannot stop it and the effect it is having on our breathing, blood pressure and perhaps the growing addictions to drink, food and to other un-healthy habits some people adopt as ways of coping.

So remember the first question of that important series of four: How am I feeling? You might add, how well am I performing? How well am I sleeping? How much am I drinking? How often do I feel genuinely relaxed, happy and calm? How long has this been going on? Do I feel as if I am behaving like the real me? Try to be as clear and truthful as possible and then follow up with the other questions: Why am I feeling this way. How do I want to feel? How will this help me? Just asking these questions might bring you to an important point of self-realisation and focus your attention on changing course and finding a way of decreasing stress levels.

As someone who regularly finds himself wide awake in the middle of the night with my mind starting to churn as I try to get back to sleep, I'd like to share one technique to do this, which I find very effective.

So how can we get back to sleep when it is clear that good, healthy sleep is surely slipping away from us? First of all we must recognise that the reason that we are awake at three in the morning is because we want to be. We want to answer the questions that are bugging us, we want to turn over and over all the concerns and worries that flood our minds and loom so large in the dark hours. So realise that a very controlling part of the brain wants to be wide awake.

Step two is to change our thinking. We can do this by thinking about something that gives us pleasure – a place that will make you relaxed. I have an imaginary log cabin in Alaska, it's in the most beautiful and peaceful setting. To become calm I can imagine every detail and free my mind to dream about this place. My advice is to think about your own special place, real or imaginary, in detail. Soon the stress levels drop and you will fall back to sleep.

The tactic of relaxation by thinking of a pleasurable place, time or person, is one we can also use beneficially during the daytime when, for example, dealing with a difficult person or situation. Creating a few moments to relax our minds will help us to think more clearly. Then we can return to the challenges before us in a healthier state of mind.

The point in all of this is that if you want to improve or build upon your health, wealth and happiness you must make a commitment to do so. If you decide to make the commitment you will prosper in your objectives by asking yourself and other people supportive questions.

Goals can be incredibly important in helping us to make a commitment and this brings us tidily back to the initial question about what we consider to be important in our lives. You may already be quite clear about the areas of your life where goals will focus your direction and assist your achievement. But not many people are. The following questions might help you to move from outline ideas to solid targets:

- What are my performance goals?
- What are my learning goals?
- What are my career goals?
- What are my financial goals?
- What are my health goals?
- What are my sharing goals?
- What are my relationship goals?
- What are my 'do before I die' goals?
- What is my most stretching goal?

If you, as do most people, have a particular concern about your finances or the way you handle money you might write down some questions to help you focus on where you stand now and where you want to be. For example:

- How much do you earn?
- How much do you want to earn?
- How much is your mortgage?
- How much would you like your mortgage to be?
- How much is your pension worth?
- How much would you like your pension to be worth?
- When would you like to retire?

- Where did you go on holiday?
- Where would you like to go on holiday?
- Where do you live?
- Where would you like to live?
- What do you drive?
- What would you like to drive?
- What would you change about your home if you could?
- If you could afford to treat yourself what would you buy?
- What else would you buy?
- If money was no object what hobby would you try?
- If money was no object what is the first thing you would buy?
- If money was no object who would you help?
- What would you do for them?
- What do you consider to be a high salary?
- What do you fear about money?
- Do you need to earn more money?
- Who do you need to help you to earn more money?
- What is the best way for you to earn more money?
- What do you need to change about yourself to earn more money?
- What do you need to know how to do to earn more money?
- What do you need to do differently?

If nothing else I hope that some of the ideas in this book have helped you to think about the last question in that list. I hope the answer to the question is, in part at least, to ask yourself and others more and better questions.

The wonderful thing about questions is that they will be a constant source of amazement and also of mental and spiritual nourishment. What more can I say?

Acknowledgements

This book really began in the early eighties when I started my first job in sales. Since then I've benefited from the wisdom of many writers, thought leaders and colleagues, too many to list here.

It has been my great privilege to see how good questions can work to improve relationships, manufacturing and services businesses, public organisations and charities.

I am deeply grateful to my clients who have opened doors for me and taught me so much. Special thanks go to Finbar Delaney, Chris Angel and Richard Webb who have been influential in the journey or producing this book.

I thank Giles Emerson, Dave Jones, Eddie Dunne, Andrew Hargreaves and my colleagues for helping me to pull together my thoughts and experiences, for editorial suggestions and encouragement in the process of producing the book.

And then there is my parents, for giving me my start and plentiful advice along the way. My wife Yvonne, children Nat and Jacob who have had to suffer the brunt of my commitments. They have inspired and supported me far more than they realise.

> *"If I had an hour to solve a problem and my life depended on the solution, I would spend the first 55 minutes determining the proper questions to ask, for once I know the proper questions I could solve the problem in less than five minutes."*
>
> ALBERT EINSTEIN

Lightning Source UK Ltd.
Milton Keynes UK
UKOW031238030213

205753UK00008B/234/P